Strengthening Math Skills
Fractions, Decimals, and Percents

Contents

Introduction

Building a solid foundation in math is a student's key to success in school and in the future. This book will help students to develop the basic math skills that they will use every day. As students build on math skills that they already know and learn new math skills, they will see how much math connects to real life.

This book will help students to:

- develop math competency;
- acquire basic math skills and concepts;
- learn problem-solving strategies;
- apply these skills and strategies to everyday life;
- gain confidence in their own ability to succeed at learning.

Students who have self-confidence in their math skills often do better in other school areas, too. Mastering math helps students to become better learners and better students.

Ensure Student Success in Math

This book contains several features that help teachers to build the self-confidence of math students. This book enables the teacher to:

- reach students by providing a unique approach to math content;
- help students build basic foundational math skills;
- diagnose specific math intervention needs;
- provide individualized, differentiated instruction.

Assessment. An assessment is included to serve as a diagnostic tool. The assessment contains most of the math concepts presented in this book. The assessment is broken into four parts. The first three parts correspond to the three units in the book. The fourth part contains word problems that emphasize various skills presented in the three units. An assessment evaluation chart helps to pinpoint each student's strengths and weaknesses. Then instruction can be focused on the math content each student needs. Each item in the assessment is linked to a lesson in the book where students can hone their math skills.

Correlation to Standards. A correlation to NCTM Standards is provided to allow teachers to tailor their teaching to standardized tests. This chart shows teachers at a glance which lessons cover the basic skills students are expected to master.

Lesson Format. Each lesson in the book is constructed to help students master the specific concept covered in the lesson. A short introduction explains the concept. Next, a step-by-step process is used to work an example problem. Students are then given a short problem to work on their own. Finally, a page of practice problems that reinforce the concept is provided.

Blackline Masters. Several blackline masters are included to allow students a better grasp of math concepts. Included are a fraction table, fraction circles, and equivalents.

Glossary. Math has a language of its own, so a glossary of math terms is included at the back of the book. Students can look up terms that confuse them, and they are directed to a specific page on which the term is explained or implemented.

Answer Key. Finally, a complete answer key is provided at the end of the book. The answer key includes the answers for the practice problems as well as explanations of how many of the answers are reached. These explanations can be useful to the teacher to explain why students might have answered incorrectly.

Working Together to Help Students Achieve

No student wants to do poorly. There are many reasons students may be having problems with math. This book presents a well-organized, straightforward approach to helping students overcome the obstacles that may hold them back. This book and your instruction can help students to regain their footing and continue their climb to math achievement.

Fractions, Decimals, and Percents: Introduction
Strengthening Math Skills, SV 9781419039027

Content Strands	**Lesson**
Number and Operations	
• understand the place-value structure of the base-ten number system and be able to represent and compare whole numbers and decimals	27, 28, 29, 30, 31, 32, 33, 34, 35, 36, 37, 38, 39, 40, 41, 42, 43, 44, 45, 46, 47, 48, 49, 50, 51, 52, 53
• develop understanding of fractions as parts of unit wholes, as parts of a collection, as locations on number lines, and as divisions of whole numbers	1, 2, 3, 4, 6, 9, 10, 11, 12, 13, 14, 15, 16, 17, 18, 19, 20, 21, 22, 23, 24, 25, 26, 29, 42, 43, 46, 47
• use models, benchmarks, and equivalent forms to judge the size of fractions	1, 2, 3, 4, 6, 8, 9, 10, 11, 12, 14, 15, 17, 18, 19, 20, 21, 22, 25, 26, 29, 42, 43, 46, 47
• recognize and generate equivalent forms of commonly used fractions, decimals, and percents	4, 5, 6, 7, 8, 9, 10, 11, 12, 14, 15, 16, 17, 18, 19, 20, 21, 22, 25, 26, 27, 28, 29, 30, 31, 32, 33, 34, 35, 36, 37, 38, 39, 40, 41, 42, 43, 44, 45, 46, 47, 48, 49, 50, 51, 52, 53
• describe classes of numbers according to characteristics such as the nature of their factors	5, 6, 7, 8, 9

Measurement	
• understand such attributes as length, area, weight, volume, and size of angle and select the appropriate type of unit for measuring each attribute	24
• understand the need for measuring with standard units and become familiar with standard units in the customary and metric systems	23, 24

Algebra	
• describe, extend, and make generalizations about geometric and numeric patterns	25, 26, 51, 53

Assessment

Part 1: Fractions

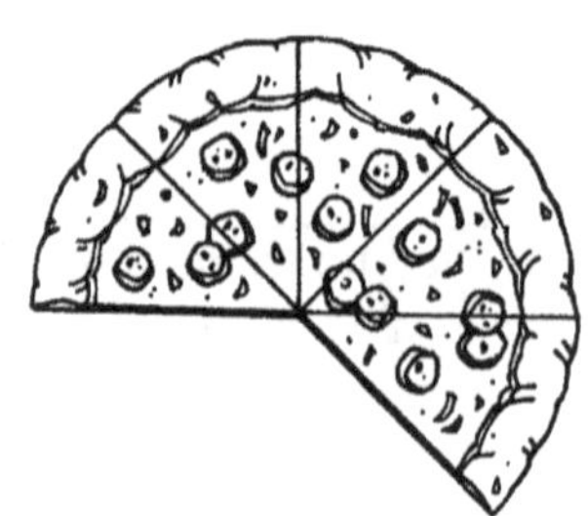

Write a fraction for each sentence.

1. Two of 5 parts were finished. _________

2. Lawrence cut the pizza into 8 pieces and ate 3 of them. _________

Write each fraction in simplest form.

3. $\frac{4}{6}$ _________

4. $\frac{2}{4}$ _________

5. $\frac{6}{10}$ _________

6. $\frac{6}{8}$ _________

7. $\frac{3}{9}$ _________

8. $\frac{6}{12}$ _________

Find the least common denominator (LCD).

9. $\frac{1}{3}$ and $\frac{1}{6}$ _________

10. $\frac{1}{2}$ and $\frac{3}{4}$ _________

11. $\frac{1}{4}$ and $\frac{5}{8}$ _________

Compare the fractions. Write <, >, or =.

12. $\frac{3}{4} \bigcirc \frac{3}{5}$

13. $\frac{3}{8} \bigcirc \frac{2}{3}$

14. $\frac{5}{10} \bigcirc \frac{1}{2}$

15. $\frac{7}{8} \bigcirc \frac{5}{6}$

16. $\frac{1}{4} \bigcirc \frac{1}{3}$

17. $\frac{4}{8} \bigcirc \frac{3}{6}$

Change these improper fractions to mixed or whole numbers.

18. $\frac{7}{5} =$ _________

19. $\frac{9}{3} =$ _________

20. $\frac{11}{4} =$ _________

Assessment

Add or subtract. Simplify if possible.

21. $\frac{1}{5} + \frac{2}{5} =$ _________

22. $\frac{7}{8} - \frac{3}{8} =$ _________

23. $\frac{3}{10} + \frac{3}{10} =$ _________

24. $\frac{3}{4} + \frac{1}{8} =$ _________

25. $\frac{5}{6} - \frac{1}{3} =$ _________

26. $\frac{7}{10} - \frac{3}{5} =$ _________

27. $2\frac{1}{2} + 1\frac{1}{4} =$ _________

28. $4\frac{4}{5} - 3\frac{2}{5} =$ _________

29. $1\frac{3}{10} + 2\frac{2}{5} =$ _________

Multiply or divide. Simplify if possible.

30. $\frac{2}{3} \times \frac{2}{5} =$ _________

31. $\frac{1}{3} \div \frac{1}{2} =$ _________

32. $\frac{3}{4} \times \frac{1}{6} =$ _________

33. $\frac{1}{2} \div \frac{3}{5} =$ _________

34. $2\frac{3}{8} \times 1\frac{1}{2} =$ _________

35. $1\frac{1}{5} \times 4 =$ _________

Use the figures below to answer questions 36–38. Be sure your answer is in simplest form.

36. What is the ratio of circles to triangles?

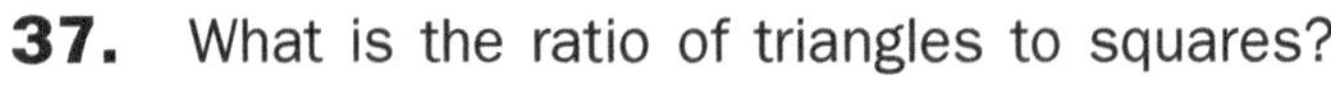

____

37. What is the ratio of triangles to squares?

____

38. What is the ratio of squares to total figures?

____

Assessment

Part 2: Decimals

Write the decimal.

1. four and four tenths _________

2. eight and twenty-five hundredths _________

Name the value of the underlined digit.

3. 7.<u>1</u> _______________

4. 4.5<u>2</u> _______________

Compare the decimals. Write <, >, or =.

5. 0.45 ◯ 0.54

6. 0.10 ◯ 0.01

7. 0.3 ◯ 0.30

8. 0.27 ◯ 0.26

9. 0.19 ◯ 0.20

10. 1.5 ◯ 1.50

Add or subtract.

11. 0.67 + 0.12 = _______

12. 0.98 − 0.46 = _______

13. 0.5 + 1.22 = _______

14. 1.51 + 0.09 = _______

15. 3.87 − 1.89 = _______

16. 4.1 − 2.39 = _______

17. $1.25 + $0.57 = _______

18. $12.34 − $8.75 = _______

19. $9.95 + $1.19 = _______

Multiply or divide.

20. 0.5 × 2 = _______

21. 9.9 ÷ 3 = _______

22. 2.7 × 10 = _______

23. 3.1 ÷ 10 = _______

24. 4.2 × 0.6 = _______

25. 5.8 × 1.1 = _______

26. $1.19 × 7 = _______

27. $6.40 ÷ 4 = _______

28. $3.25 × 5 = _______

Assessment

Part 3: Percents

Complete.

1. Ratio = $\frac{47}{100}$

Decimal = 0.47

Percent = __________

2. Ratio = $\frac{85}{100}$

Decimal = 0.85

Percent = __________

3. Ratio = $\frac{123}{100}$

Decimal = 1.23

Percent = __________

Write each decimal as a percent. Remember to add the percent symbol.

4. 0.35 = __________

5. 0.19 = __________

6. 2.50 = __________

Write each percent as a decimal. Remember to remove the percent symbol and add the decimal point.

7. 54% = __________

8. 88% = __________

9. 2% = __________

Write each fraction as a percent. Add zeros if needed. Remember to add the percent symbol.

10. $\frac{7}{10}$ = __________

11. $\frac{1}{4}$ = __________

12. $\frac{1}{2}$ = __________

Write each percent as a fraction. Simplify if possible.

13. 30% = __________

14. 80% = __________

15. 55% = __________

Use the percent triangle to find the part.

16. 50% of 600 = __________

17. 30% of 210 = __________

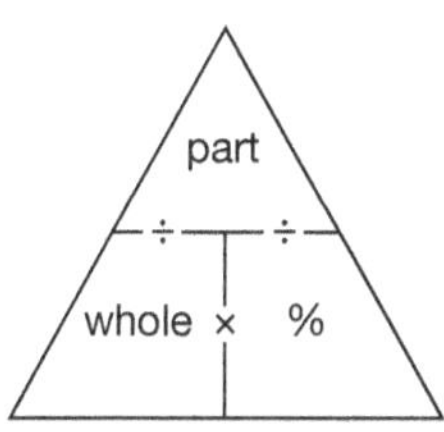

Use the percent triangle to find the whole.

18. 25 is 25% of what number? __________

19. 16 is 40% of what number? __________

Use the percent triangle to find the percent.

20. 70 is what percent of 100? __________

21. 38 is what percent of 76? __________

Assessment

Part 4: Word Problems

Solve.

1. Ming used $\frac{2}{3}$ cup of raisins in her recipe. Liz used $\frac{5}{8}$ cup of raisins in her recipe. Which girl used more raisins?

2. It takes Ming 40 minutes to bake her raisin bread. In simplest form, what part of an hour is 40 minutes?

3. Of the 24 hours in each day, Kisha spends $\frac{1}{3}$ of them sleeping. How many hours does she sleep each day?

4. Some scouts hiked along a trail. On the first day, they hiked $\frac{2}{8}$ of the trail. On the second day, they hiked $\frac{3}{8}$ of the trail. What part of the trail did they hike during the two days?

5. A bicycle race is $2\frac{2}{3}$ miles long. The race is held on a track that is $\frac{1}{3}$ mile long. How many times must the racers go around the track to complete the race?

6. Donna completed the bicycle race in 12.4 minutes. Juan completed the race in 11.95 minutes. How much faster was Juan's time?

7. A store sells one package of socks for $4.69 or 2 packages for $9.25. Which is the better buy?

8. Brett began the day with $10.75. She bought lunch for $4.83, a snack for $0.97, and a book for $2.95. How much money did Brett have left at the end of the day?

9. There are 260 students at Dylan's school. Of these, 75% have a pet. How many of the students have a pet?

10. Nick started a savings account. He put $300.00 in the account with an interest rate of 4%. How much money would Nick have in the account after 1 year?

Assessment Evaluation Chart

Circle the number of each assessment item that you missed. Then use the Lesson Review list to find more practice problems.

ITEM NUMBERS	LESSON FOR REVIEW	ITEM NUMBER	LESSON FOR REVIEW
Part 1: Fractions		**Part 3: Percents**	
1, 2	Lessons 1, 2	1–3	Lesson 42
3–8	Lesson 6	4–6	Lesson 44
9–11	Lessons 7, 8	7–9	Lesson 45
12–17	Lesson 9	10–12	Lesson 46
18–20	Lesson 11	13–15	Lesson 47
21,23	Lesson 13	16, 17	Lesson 48
22	Lesson 16	18, 19	Lesson 49
24	Lesson 14	20, 21	Lesson 50
25, 26	Lesson 17	**Part 4: Word Problems**	
27, 29	Lesson 15	1	Lesson 9
28	Lesson 18	2	Lesson 23
30, 32	Lesson 19	3	Lesson 20
31, 33	Lesson 22	4	Lesson 13
34	Lesson 21	5	Lesson 22
35	Lesson 20	6	Lesson 33
36–38	Lesson 26	7	Lesson 41
Part 2: Decimals		8	Lesson 40
1, 2	Lesson 27	9	Lesson 48
3, 4	Lesson 28	10	Lesson 53
5–10	Lesson 31		
11, 13, 14	Lesson 32		
12, 15, 16	Lesson 33		
17–19	Lesson 40		
20	Lesson 34		
21	Lesson 38		
22	Lesson 35		
23	Lesson 39		
24, 25	Lesson 36		
26–28	Lesson 41		

LESSON 1   What Is a Fraction?

A **fraction** is a number that names equal parts of a whole.

Three of the 5 parts of the rectangle are shaded. You can say that $\frac{3}{5}$, or three fifths, of the rectangle is shaded.

Example

What fraction of the rectangle is shaded?

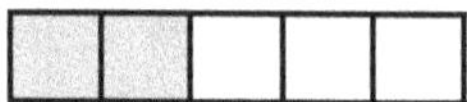

STEP 1 Name the total number of pieces.

The total number of pieces is the whole. The rectangle is divided into a total of 5 parts. That number goes on the bottom of the fraction.

STEP 2 Name the number of pieces that are shaded.

The part of the whole is the numerator. There are 2 parts shaded. That number goes on the top of the fraction.

STEP 3 Write the fraction.

$$\frac{\text{part}}{\text{whole}} = \frac{2}{5}$$

So, $\frac{2}{5}$ of the rectangle is shaded.

(ON YOUR OWN)

What part of the circle is shaded? Write the fraction.

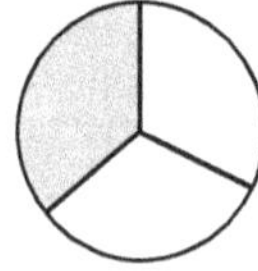

Fractions, Decimals, and Percents: Unit 1: Lesson 1
Strengthening Math Skills, SV 9781419039027

Practice

Building Skills

What part of the whole is shaded? Write the fraction.

> The top number in a fraction is the part. The bottom number is the whole.

1. 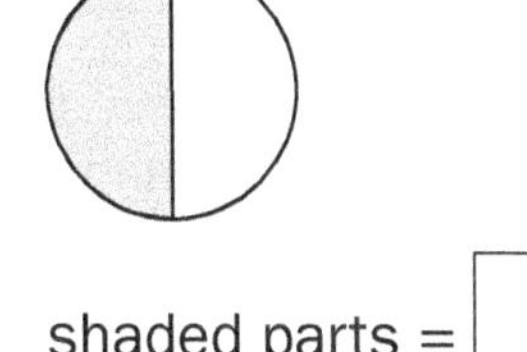

shaded parts = ☐
total parts = ☐

2. 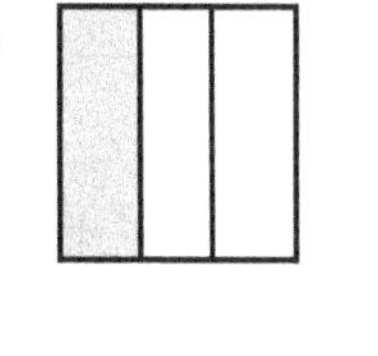

shaded parts = ☐
total parts = ☐

3. 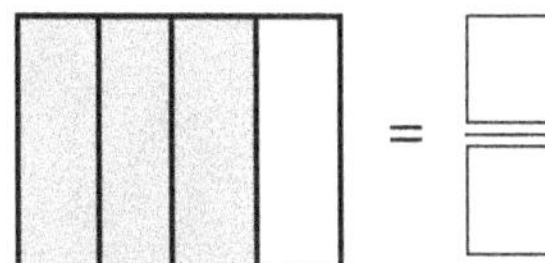 = ☐/☐

4. 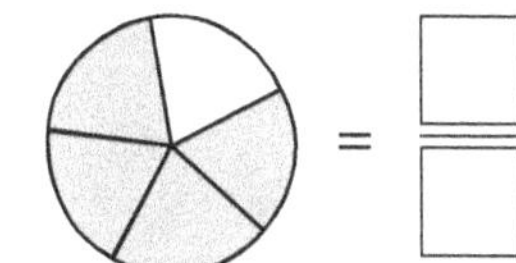 = ☐/☐

Problem Solving

Solve. Write a fraction.

5. Jason cut a melon into 6 pieces. Jason ate 1 piece. What fraction of the melon was eaten?

6. Erin's mother cut a pie into 8 pieces. Five of the pieces were eaten. What fraction of the pie was <u>not</u> eaten?

7. Laronda's birthday cake was cut into 10 pieces. Seven of the pieces were eaten at her birthday party. What fraction of the cake was eaten?

8. Ten dimes make a dollar. What fraction of a dollar is 1 dime?

LESSON ❷ Writing Fractions

A fraction names equal parts of a whole. The top number, or **numerator**, tells how many parts are being used. The bottom number, or **denominator**, tells how many equal parts there are in all. Fractions can also be written as words.

Example

A pizza is cut into 6 equal pieces. Jenna eats 2 pieces. Write a fraction to show the part of the pizza that is left.

STEP 1 Name the denominator.

The total number of pieces is the whole. The pizza is cut into a total of 6 pieces, so the denominator is 6.

STEP 2 Name the numerator.

The number of pieces left is the part of the whole. There are 4 pieces of pizza left, so the numerator is 4.

STEP 3 Write the fraction.

$$\frac{\text{part}}{\text{whole}} = \frac{4}{6} = \text{four sixths}$$

So, $\frac{4}{6}$ or four sixths of the pizza is left.

(**ON YOUR OWN**)

Jenna cut her pancake into 4 equal parts. She ate 3 of the parts. What part of the pancake is left? Write a fraction in numbers and words.

Practice

> The numerator names the part. The denominator names the whole.

Building Skills

How much of each figure is shaded? Write the fraction.

1. 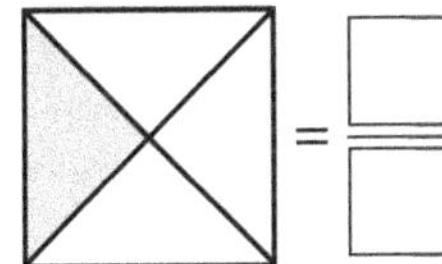

2. 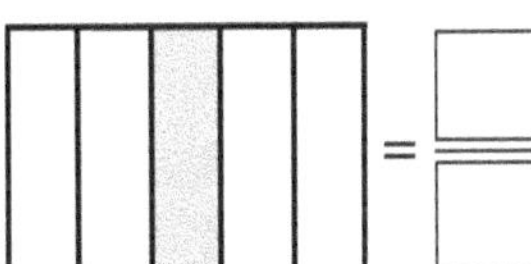

3. 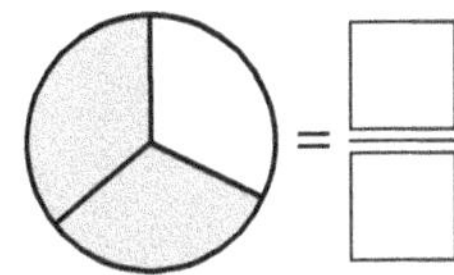

4. 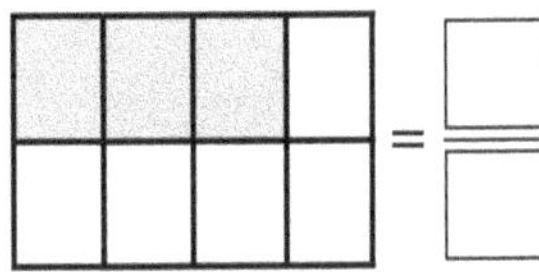

Write words to name each fraction.

5. $\frac{1}{4}$ = _______________

6. $\frac{4}{5}$ = _______________

7. $\frac{2}{3}$ = _______________

8. $\frac{5}{8}$ = _______________

Problem Solving

Solve. Write a fraction.

9. Mr. Seed divided his backyard into 8 equal parts. He mowed 7 of the parts. What fraction of his yard did Mr. Seed mow? Write a fraction in numbers and words.

10. Emma divided a poster board into 6 equal parts. She painted 5 of the parts. What fraction of the poster board did Emma paint? Write a fraction in numbers and words.

LESSON 3 · Part of a Group

A fraction can also name equal parts of a group. The numerator tells how many parts are being used. The denominator tells how many parts there are in all in the group.

Example

What fraction of the group is shaded?

STEP 1 Name the denominator.

The denominator tells how many are in the group. There are 5 triangles altogether, so the denominator is 5.

STEP 2 Name the numerator.

The numerator tells how many parts are being used. There are 3 triangles shaded, so the numerator is 3.

STEP 3 Write the fraction.

$$\frac{\text{parts}}{\text{group}} = \frac{3}{5} = \text{three fifths}$$

So, $\frac{3}{5}$ or **three fifths of the triangles are shaded.**

ON YOUR OWN

What fraction of the group is shaded? Write a fraction in numbers and words.

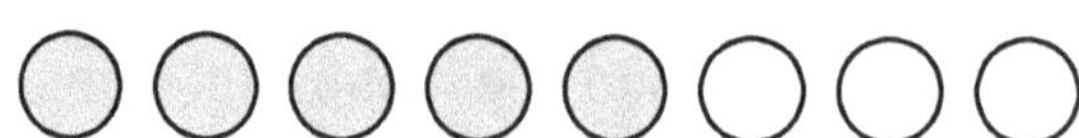

Practice

Building Skills

> The numerator tells how many parts are being used. The denominator tells how many are in the group.

What fraction of the group is shaded? Write the fraction.

1. ⬤ ◯ ◯

$$\frac{\text{shaded parts}}{\text{total in group}} = \frac{\Box}{\Box}$$

2. ★ ☆ ☆ ☆

$$\frac{\text{shaded parts}}{\text{total in group}} = \frac{\Box}{\Box}$$

3. △ △ △ △ △ △

$$\frac{\Box}{\Box}$$

4. ▢ ▢ ▢ ▢ ▢ ▢ ▢ ▢

$$\frac{\Box}{\Box}$$

Problem Solving

Solve. Write a fraction.

5. What fraction of the fruits are apples?

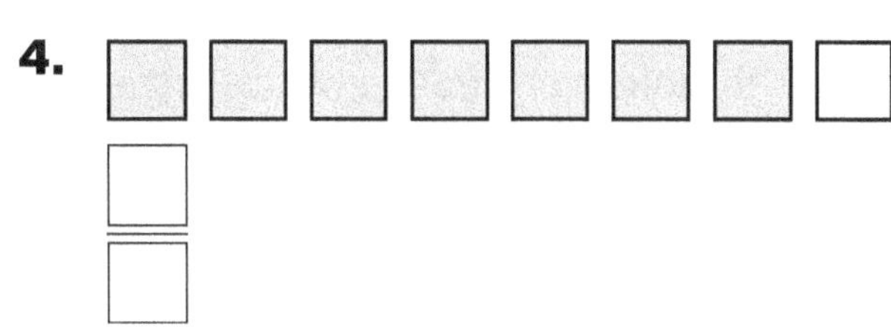

6. What fraction of the fruits are <u>not</u> apples?

7. Two of the 3 pets in the backyard are dogs. What fraction of the pets in the backyard are dogs? Write the fraction as a number and as words.

8. There are 8 horses living on a ranch. Of these, 5 are female. What part of the horses are females?

LESSON 4 Equivalent Fractions

You can use different fractions to name the same amount. Fractions that name the same amount are known as **equivalent fractions.** *Equivalent* means equal in value.

Look at the squares. They are the same size.

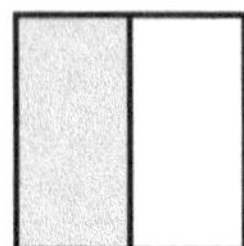

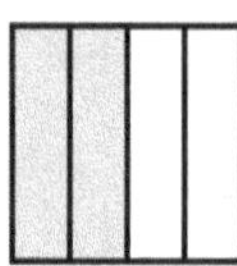

The shaded part is $\frac{1}{2}$ of the square.   The shaded part is $\frac{2}{4}$ of the square.

You can see that $\frac{1}{2}$ and $\frac{2}{4}$ name the same amount. So, $\frac{1}{2}$ and $\frac{2}{4}$ are equivalent fractions.

- To find an equivalent fraction with bigger numbers, multiply both the numerator and denominator by the same number.

- To find an equivalent fraction with smaller numbers, divide both the numerator and the denominator by the same number.

Example

Divide both the numerator and denominator to find an equivalent fraction for $\frac{8}{10}$.

STEP 1 Divide the numerator by 2. $8 \div 2 = 4$

STEP 2 Divide the denominator by 2. $10 \div 2 = 5$

STEP 3 Write the equivalent fractions.

$$\frac{8}{10} = \frac{4}{5}$$

So, $\frac{8}{10}$ and $\frac{4}{5}$ are equivalent fractions.

ON YOUR OWN

Multiply both the numerator and the denominator by the same number to find an equivalent fraction for $\frac{2}{3}$.

Practice

Test each strategy for the easiest way to find an equivalent fraction.

Building Skills

Decide if the fractions are equivalent. Write *yes* or *no*. Show your work.

1. $\frac{1}{3} = \frac{2}{6}$ _________

2. $\frac{1}{2} = \frac{3}{8}$ _________

Multiply both the numerator and denominator by the same number to find an equivalent fraction. Show your work.

3. $\frac{3}{4} =$ _________

4. $\frac{3}{5} =$ _________

Divide both the numerator and denominator by the same number to find an equivalent fraction. Show your work.

5. $\frac{6}{10} =$ _________

6. $\frac{12}{16} =$ _________

Problem Solving

Solve.

7. Angela has worked 9 of her 12 math problems. Write a fraction that names the number of problems she has worked. Then write an equivalent fraction.

_________ = _________

8. Pablo invited 16 people to his party, and 10 of them came. Write a fraction that names how many of the invited people came to the party. Then write an equivalent fraction.

_________ = _________

LESSON 5 Greatest Common Factor

Factors are the numbers multiplied together to form a product. The greatest factor that two or more numbers have in common is the **greatest common factor**, or **GCF**. For example, the greatest common factor of 4 and 6 is 2.

Example

Find the greatest common factor of 8 and 12.

STEP 1 Find the factors of each number. Use a factor tree to help you.

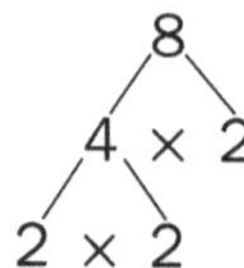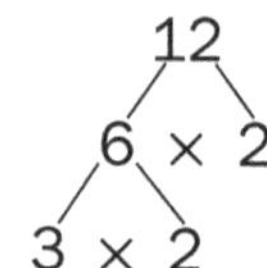

STEP 2 Find the factors that are the same for both numbers.

$$8 = 2 \times \boxed{2} \times \boxed{2}$$
$$12 = 3 \times \boxed{2} \times \boxed{2}$$

STEP 3 Multiply the common factors.

$$2 \times 2 = 4$$

So, the greatest common factor of 8 and 12 is 4.

ON YOUR OWN

Draw a factor tree to find the greatest common factor of 4 and 8. Show your work.

Practice

Building Skills

Complete each step to find the greatest common factor for the given numbers.

1. 6 and 18

STEP 1

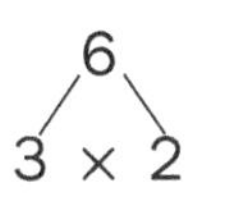
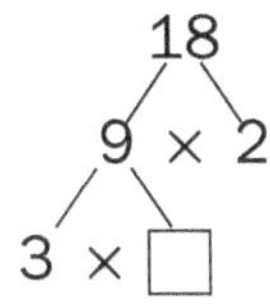

STEP 2

6 = 3 × 2
18 = 3 × ☐ × ☐

STEP 3

☐ × ☐ = ☐
The GCF is __________.

2. 6 and 12

STEP 1

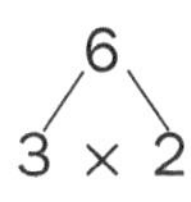
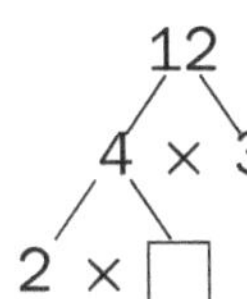

STEP 2

6 = 3 × 2
12 = 3 × ☐ × ☐

STEP 3

☐ × ☐ = ☐
The GCF is __________.

Problem Solving

Solve. Show your work on another sheet of paper.

3. What is the GCF of 4 and 8?

GCF = ______________

4. What is the GCF of 9 and 12?

GCF = ______________

5. What is the GCF of 8 and 16?

GCF = ______________

6. What is the GCF of 5 and 20?

GCF = ______________

7. The GCF of two numbers is 3. Added together, the two numbers equal 9. What are the two numbers?

8. The GCF of two numbers is 1. Added together, the two numbers equal 3. What are the two numbers?

LESSON 6 Simplest Form

A fraction is in **simplest form,** or lowest terms, when the greatest common factor (GCF) of the numerator and denominator is 1. To simplify a fraction, divide the numerator and denominator by the same number.

$\frac{1}{2}$ and $\frac{7}{9}$ are in simplest form. $\frac{2}{4}$ and $\frac{6}{9}$ are not in simplest form.

Example

Write $\frac{4}{8}$ in its simplest form.

STEP 1 Find the factors for the two numbers.

$$4 \quad\quad 8$$
$$2 \times 2 \quad\quad 2 \times 4$$
$$2 \times 2$$

STEP 2 Find the GCF of the two numbers.

$$4 = \boxed{2} \times \boxed{2}$$
$$8 = \boxed{2} \times \boxed{2} \times 2$$

$$2 \times 2 = 4 \quad\quad \text{The GCF is 4.}$$

STEP 3 Divide the numerator and denominator by the GCF.

$$\frac{4}{8} = \frac{4 \div 4}{8 \div 4} = \frac{1}{2}$$

So, $\frac{4}{8}$ written in simplest form is $\frac{1}{2}$.
$\frac{4}{8}$ and $\frac{1}{2}$ name the same value.

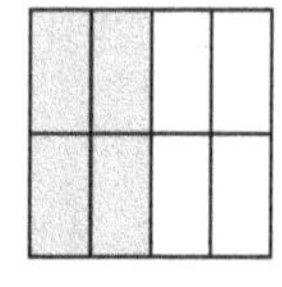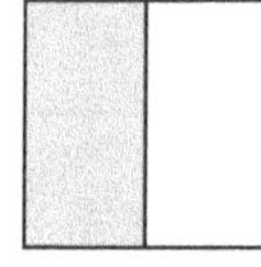

$$\frac{4}{8} \quad\quad\quad \frac{1}{2}$$

ON YOUR OWN

Write the fraction $\frac{3}{6}$ in its simplest form. **Show your work on another sheet of paper.**

Practice

> Divide the numerator and denominator by the same number to simplify a fraction.

Building Skills

Write each fraction in simplest form.

1. 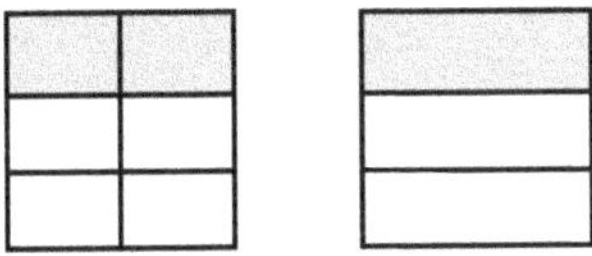

$$\frac{2}{6} = \frac{2 \div 2}{6 \div 2} = \frac{\boxed{}}{\boxed{}}$$

2. 

$$\frac{8}{10} = \frac{\boxed{}}{\boxed{}}$$

3. $\dfrac{6}{12} = \dfrac{6 \div 6}{12 \div 6} = \dfrac{\boxed{}}{2}$

4. $\dfrac{4}{16} = \dfrac{4 \div 4}{16 \div 4} = \dfrac{1}{\boxed{}}$

5. $\dfrac{4}{6} = $ _________

6. $\dfrac{3}{9} = $ _________

7. $\dfrac{5}{10} = $ _________

8. $\dfrac{6}{8} = $ _________

Problem Solving

Solve.

9. Kaytee painted her bedroom. It took her 8 hours. She spent 4 hours painting her ceiling. What fraction of her time did she spend painting her ceiling? Write the fraction in simplest terms.

10. Collin collected coins. He had 10 quarters in his collection. Four of his quarters were silver. What fraction of Collin's quarters were silver? Write the fraction in simplest terms.

Fractions, Decimals, and Percents: Unit 1: Lesson 6
Strengthening Math Skills, SV 9781419039027

LESSON 7 — Least Common Multiple

The product of two or more numbers is a **multiple.** Multiples of one number can also be multiples of another number. Then the multiples are called **common multiples.** The smallest number that is a common multiple is known as the **least common multiple,** or **LCM.** You will use least common multiples to compare fractions.

Example

Find the least common multiple of 4 and 6.

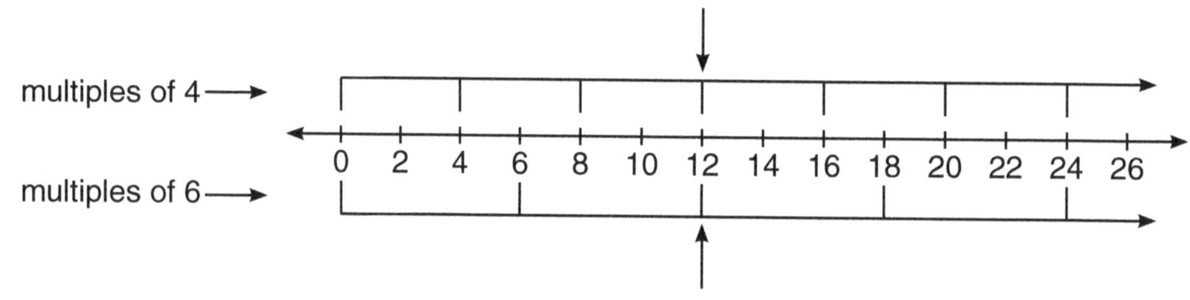

STEP 1 Find the multiples of each number. Use a number line.

STEP 2 Circle the lowest multiple the two numbers have in common.

Multiples of 4:   4   8   (12)   16   20   24 …

Multiples of 6:   6   (12)   18   24 …

So, the least common multiple of 4 and 6 is **12**.

ON YOUR OWN

Draw a number line to find the least common multiple of 3 and 5.

Least common multiple of 3 and 5 = __________

Practice

Building Skills

> Use a number line to help you find the least common multiple of two numbers.

Use the number line to find the least common multiple for each pair of numbers. Write the least common multiple.

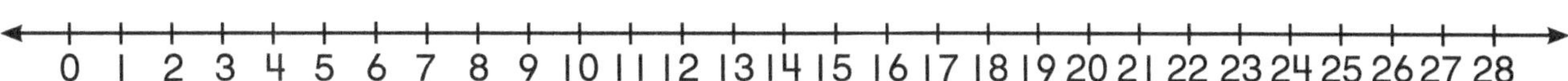

1. 2 and 3

    LCM = _____________

2. 3 and 4

    LCM = _____________

3. 4 and 5

    LCM = _____________

4. 4 and 7

    LCM = _____________

5. 3 and 6

    LCM = _____________

6. 6 and 8

    LCM = _____________

Problem Solving

Solve.

7. Cal has karate class every 3 days. Carla has karate class every 4 days. If they both practice today, in how many days will they both practice on the same day again?

8. Nikki goes to dance practice every second day. Allison goes to dance practice every fifth day. If they both went to practice today, in how many days will they both go to practice again on the same day?

LESSON ⑧ Least Common Denominator

To work with fractions, you must often have fractions with the same denominator. To find the common denominator, use the least common multiple (LCM) of the denominators. This is also called the **least common denominator (LCD).** The LCD is the least common multiple of the denominator of two or more fractions.

Example

Rewrite $\frac{2}{3}$ and $\frac{1}{4}$ by using the least common denominator (LCD).

STEP 1 Find the LCM of the denominators.

Multiples of 3: 3 6 9 ⑫ 15 18

Multiples of 4: 4 8 ⑫ 16 20

The LCM of 3 and 4 is 12. So, the least common denominator (LCD) of $\frac{2}{3}$ and $\frac{1}{4}$ is 12.

STEP 2 Write the equivalent fractions using the LCD.

$$\frac{2}{3} = \frac{2 \times 4}{3 \times 4} = \frac{8}{12}$$

$$\frac{1}{4} = \frac{1 \times 3}{4 \times 3} = \frac{3}{12}$$

ON YOUR OWN

Rewrite $\frac{2}{5}$ and $\frac{1}{2}$ by using the least common denominator (LCD).

Multiples of 5:

Multiples of 2:

LCD = __________

$\frac{2}{5} =$

$\frac{1}{2} =$

Name ____ Date _____________________________

Practice

Building Skills

Write equivalent fractions for each pair of fractions using the LCD.

1. $\frac{2}{3}, \frac{3}{5}$

Find the LCM of __________ and __________.

Multiples of 3: __________ __________ __________ __________ __________

Multiples of 5: __________ __________ __________ __________ __________

The LCM of __________ and __________ is __________.

So, the LCD of $\frac{2}{3}$ and $\frac{3}{5}$ is __________.

$\frac{2}{3} = \dfrac{2 \times \boxed{}}{3 \times \boxed{}} = \dfrac{\boxed{}}{\boxed{}}$
$\qquad$
$\frac{3}{5} = \dfrac{3 \times \boxed{}}{5 \times \boxed{}} = \dfrac{\boxed{}}{\boxed{}}$

2. $\frac{3}{4}, \frac{1}{3}$ __________

3. $\frac{1}{2}, \frac{2}{3}$ __________

4. $\frac{5}{6}, \frac{1}{12}$ __________

5. $\frac{2}{7}, \frac{1}{2}$ __________

Problem Solving

Solve.

6. Jeff has two containers of paint. One is $\frac{2}{3}$ full, and the other is $\frac{3}{4}$ full. He wants to know which can has more paint. What LCD can he use to compare the two numbers? Rewrite the fractions with the LCD.

LCD = __________ $\qquad$ $\frac{2}{3} =$ __________________ $\qquad$ $\frac{3}{4} =$ __________________

7. Sali has finished $\frac{1}{3}$ of her math problems. Carlton has finished $\frac{2}{5}$ of his problems. What LCD can they use to tell who has finished more problems? Rewrite the fractions with the LCD.

LCD = __________ $\qquad$ $\frac{1}{3} =$ __________________ $\qquad$ $\frac{2}{5} =$ __________________

8. Maria has read $\frac{5}{6}$ of her book. Vince has read $\frac{4}{5}$ of his book. What LCD can they use to tell who has read more? Rewrite the fractions with the LCD.

LCD = __________ $\qquad$ $\frac{5}{6} =$ __________________ $\qquad$ $\frac{4}{5} =$ __________________

LESSON 9 Comparing Fractions

You can **compare** fractions that have the same denominators. When the denominators are the same, compare the numerators to see which fraction is greater. The fraction with the greater numerator is the greater fraction.

$\frac{2}{5}$ $\frac{3}{5}$

$$\frac{2}{5} < \frac{3}{5} \qquad \text{or} \qquad \frac{3}{5} > \frac{2}{5}$$

Use the symbol < to mean "is less than." $\frac{1}{4} < \frac{3}{4}$

Use the symbol > to mean "is greater than." $\frac{3}{4} > \frac{1}{4}$

Use the symbol = to mean "equals." $\frac{2}{4} = \frac{1}{2}$

You can also compare fractions that have different denominators.

Example

Compare $\frac{1}{2}$ and $\frac{2}{3}$. Use <, >, or = signs. $\frac{1}{2}$

STEP 1 Find the least common denominator (LCD).

Multiples of 2:   2   4   ⑥   8 ...

Multiples of 3:   3   ⑥   9   12 ... $\frac{2}{3}$

The least common multiple (LCM) of the denominators is 6. So, the LCD is 6.

STEP 2 Write equivalent fractions using the LCD as the new denominator.

$$\frac{1 \times 3}{2 \times 3} = \frac{3}{6} \qquad\qquad \frac{2 \times 2}{3 \times 2} = \frac{4}{6}$$

STEP 3 Compare the numerators.

$$3 < 4, \text{ so } \frac{3}{6} < \frac{4}{6}, \text{ so } \frac{1}{2} < \frac{2}{3}$$

ON YOUR OWN

Candace has finished $\frac{3}{5}$ of her homework. Brittan has finished $\frac{2}{3}$ of his homework. Use <, >, or = to show who has completed more of the homework.

Practice

> To compare fractions, first find the LCD, and then compare the numerators.

Building Skills

Compare. Write <, >, or =.

1. 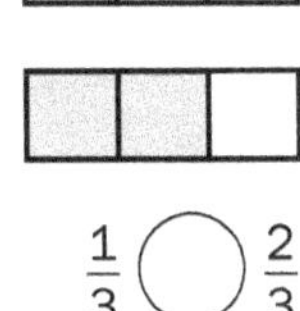

$\dfrac{1}{3} \bigcirc \dfrac{2}{3}$

2. 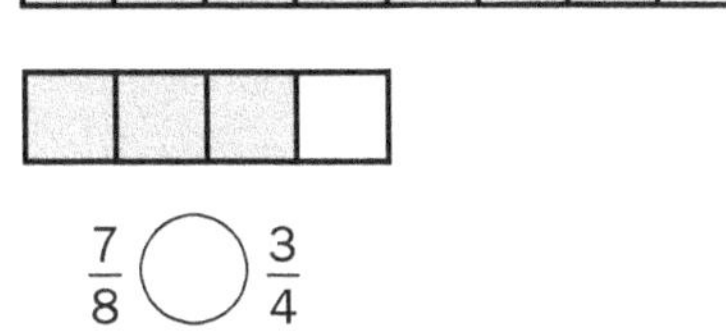

$\dfrac{7}{8} \bigcirc \dfrac{3}{4}$

Compare. Write <, >, or =.

3. $\dfrac{4}{5} \bigcirc \dfrac{3}{5}$

4. $\dfrac{1}{4} \bigcirc \dfrac{2}{4}$

5. $\dfrac{1}{2} \bigcirc \dfrac{1}{5}$

6. $\dfrac{1}{3} \bigcirc \dfrac{1}{4}$

7. $\dfrac{5}{6} \bigcirc \dfrac{3}{4}$

8. $\dfrac{3}{8} \bigcirc \dfrac{3}{4}$

Problem Solving

Solve.

9. Leesa studied for $\dfrac{2}{3}$ hour. Monroe studied for $\dfrac{3}{4}$ hour. Who studied longer?

10. Carri rode her bike $\dfrac{3}{5}$ of a mile. Jacob rode his bike $\dfrac{1}{2}$ of a mile. Cho rode his bike $\dfrac{7}{10}$ of a mile. Who traveled the farthest?

LESSON **10** **Mixed Numbers**

A **mixed number** is made up of a whole number and a fraction, such as $3\frac{2}{3}$.

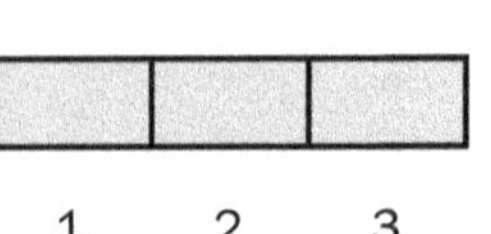 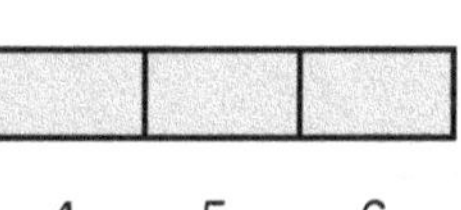 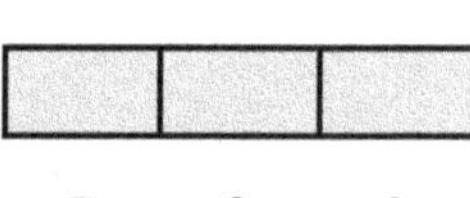

$\frac{1}{3}$ $\frac{2}{3}$ $\frac{3}{3}$ $\frac{4}{3}$ $\frac{5}{3}$ $\frac{6}{3}$ $\frac{7}{3}$ $\frac{8}{3}$ $\frac{9}{3}$ $\frac{10}{3}$ $\frac{11}{3}$

There are 3 whole figures shaded. The last figure is $\frac{2}{3}$ shaded. So, $3\frac{2}{3}$ figures are shaded. You can also say that $\frac{11}{3}$ of the figures are shaded.

Example

Write a mixed number to name the shaded part of the figures.

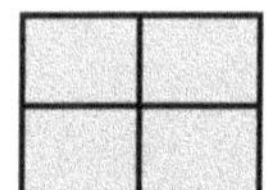 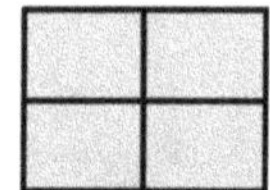 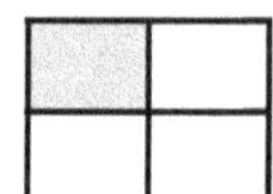

STEP 1 Count the number of squares that are completely shaded.

Two squares are completely shaded. 2 is the whole number in the mixed number.

STEP 2 Count the number of parts in the square that is not completely shaded.

The last square is divided into 4 equal parts. 1 of the 4 parts is shaded. $\frac{1}{4}$ is the fraction in the mixed number.

STEP 3 Write the mixed number.

$$2 + \frac{1}{4} = 2\frac{1}{4}$$

So, $2\frac{1}{4}$ of the figures are shaded.

ON YOUR OWN

Write a mixed number to name the shaded part of the figures.

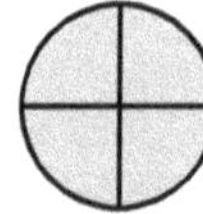 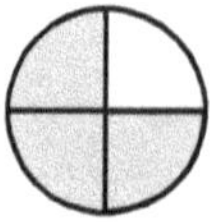

Practice

Mixed numbers contain a whole number and a fraction.

Building Skills

Write a mixed number to name the shaded part of the figures.

1. 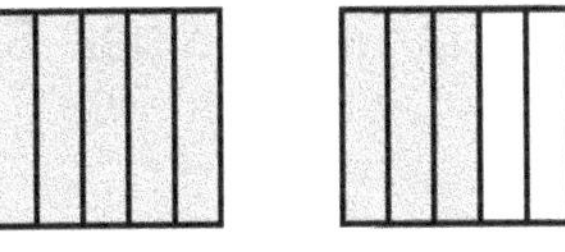

____

2. 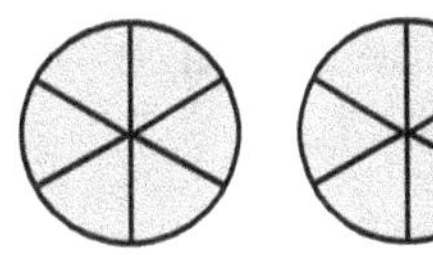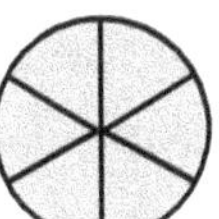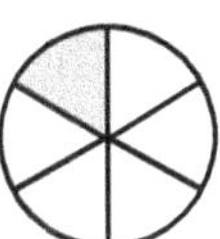

____

3. 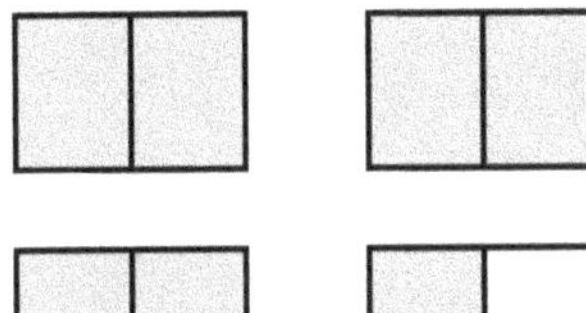

____

4. 

____

Problem Solving

Solve. Write a mixed number.

5. Janelle had 3 pizzas at her birthday party. Each pizza was cut into 6 pieces. At the end of the party, 5 pieces of pizza were left. Write a mixed number to name how much of the pizzas was eaten.

6. For the class picnic, Mrs. Samson brought 2 watermelons. Each watermelon was cut into 10 equal pieces. At the end of the picnic, 3 pieces of watermelon were left. Write a mixed number to name how much of the watermelons was eaten.

Fractions, Decimals, and Percents: Unit 1: Lesson 10
Strengthening Math Skills, SV 9781419039027

LESSON ⓫ Improper Fractions

An **improper fraction** is a fraction with a numerator *equal to* or *greater than* its denominator. For example, $\frac{11}{3}$ and $\frac{10}{10}$ are improper fractions.

You change an improper fraction to a mixed number or whole number by dividing. The denominator of the improper fraction becomes the denominator of the mixed number. Simplify a mixed number if possible.

Example

Write $\frac{14}{4}$ as a mixed number.

$\frac{14}{4}$ are shaded.

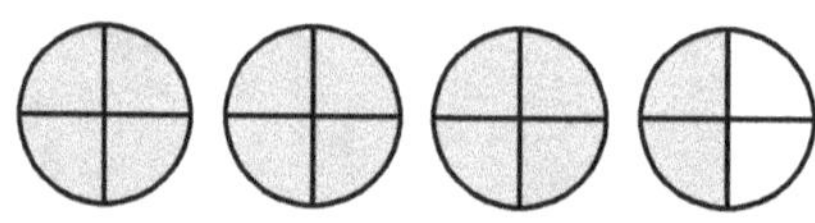

STEP 1 Divide the numerator by the denominator.

$$\begin{array}{r} 3 \\ 4\overline{)14} \\ -12 \\ \hline 2 \end{array}$$

STEP 2 Show how many fourths are left over.

$$3\frac{2}{4} \leftarrow \text{remainder}$$
$$\phantom{3\frac{2}{4}} \leftarrow \text{divisor}$$
$$\begin{array}{r} 4\overline{)14} \\ -12 \\ \hline 2 \end{array}$$

So, the improper fraction $\frac{14}{4}$ = the mixed number $3\frac{2}{4}$. The mixed number can be simplified.

$$\frac{14}{4} = 3\frac{2}{4} = 3\frac{1}{2}$$

ON YOUR OWN

Write $\frac{7}{2}$ as a mixed number. Simplify if possible.

$$\frac{7}{2} = \underline{\hspace{3cm}}$$

Practice

Building Skills

Rename each improper fraction as a mixed number or whole number. Simplify if possible.

1. $\frac{3}{2} =$ _____________

2. $\frac{7}{3} =$ _____________

3. $\frac{11}{4} =$ _____________

4. $\frac{9}{5} =$ _____________

5. $\frac{13}{6} =$ _____________

6. $\frac{15}{8} =$ _____________

7. $\frac{10}{4} =$ _____________

8. $\frac{14}{7} =$ _____________

9. $\frac{14}{8} =$ _____________

Problem Solving

Solve.

10. Kayla walked $\frac{6}{4}$ hours. Rewrite this improper fraction as a mixed number or whole number. Simplify if possible.

11. How many pairs of socks can be made from a pile of 11 socks? Write the answer as an improper fraction and then as a mixed number or whole number. Simplify if possible.

12. Victor's family went on vacation. They drove for $\frac{20}{4}$ hours. Rewrite this improper fraction as a mixed number or whole number. Simplify if possible.

LESSON 12 — Changing Mixed Numbers or Whole Numbers to Improper Fractions

A mixed number is made up of a whole number and a fraction. For example, $1\frac{4}{5}$ is a mixed number.

An improper fraction is a fraction with a numerator *equal to* or *greater than* its denominator. For example, $\frac{9}{5}$ and $\frac{8}{4}$ are improper fractions.

You can rename a mixed number as an improper fraction. You change a mixed number to an improper fraction by multiplying. The denominator of the mixed number becomes the denominator of the improper fraction.

$$1\frac{4}{5} = \frac{9}{5}$$

A whole number can also be renamed as an improper fraction. When a whole number is renamed as an improper fraction, the denominator will be 1.

$$3 = \frac{3}{1}$$

Example

Write $3\frac{1}{3}$ as an improper fraction.

STEP 1 Multiply the denominator by the whole number.

$$3 \times 3 = 9$$

STEP 2 Add the numerator.

$$9 + 1 = 10$$

STEP 3 Write that total as the numerator. Keep the denominator the same.

$$\frac{10}{3}$$

So, $3\frac{1}{3}$ written as an improper fraction is $\frac{10}{3}$.

ON YOUR OWN

Write $2\frac{2}{3}$ as an improper fraction.

$$2\frac{2}{3} = \underline{\hspace{3cm}}$$

Practice

Building Skills

Rename each mixed number or whole number as an improper fraction. Simplify if possible.

1. $2\frac{1}{2} =$ __________

2. $4\frac{1}{5} =$ __________

3. $1\frac{3}{4} =$ __________

4. $7 =$ __________

5. $1\frac{3}{8} =$ __________

6. $3\frac{3}{5} =$ __________

7. $1\frac{1}{10} =$ __________

8. $10 =$ __________

9. $5\frac{2}{5} =$ __________

Problem Solving

Solve.

10. Tony must add $2\frac{1}{4}$ quarts of oil to a customer's car engine. Change $2\frac{1}{4}$ to an improper fraction.

11. The baseball game was stopped after $5\frac{1}{2}$ innings. Change $5\frac{1}{2}$ to an improper fraction.

12. Tex has $3\frac{1}{2}$ yards of rope. Change $3\frac{1}{2}$ to an improper fraction.

13. Bob's band practiced for $1\frac{1}{4}$ hours. Change $1\frac{1}{4}$ to an improper fraction.

14. Leda bought $1\frac{5}{8}$ pounds of potato salad. Change $1\frac{5}{8}$ to an improper fraction.

LESSON 13 — Adding Fractions with Like Denominators

Like fractions are fractions that have the same denominator. Because $\frac{1}{5}$ and $\frac{3}{5}$ have the same denominator, they are like fractions. When the denominators are the same, adding fractions is easy.

To add like fractions, add only the numerators.

$$\frac{\text{numerator} + \text{numerator}}{\text{denominator}} \qquad \frac{1}{5} + \frac{3}{5} = \frac{1+3}{5} = \frac{4}{5}$$

To add like fractions, add the numerators but not the denominators. After you add, check that the answer is in the simplest form.

Example

Add. $\frac{1}{2} + \frac{1}{2} =$ _________ Simplify your answer if possible.

STEP 1 Add the numerators. $\frac{1+1}{2} = \frac{2}{2}$

STEP 2 Simplify if possible. $\frac{2}{2} = 1$

$\frac{2}{2}$ is an improper fraction that equals the whole number 1.

So, $\frac{1}{2} + \frac{1}{2} = 1$

ON YOUR OWN

Jessica sang for $\frac{1}{4}$ hour in the morning and $\frac{1}{4}$ hour in the afternoon. How long did she sing in all? Simplify your answer if possible.

Practice

Building Skills

> To add like fractions, add only the numerators.

Shade the correct number of parts. Then solve.

1. $\frac{2}{4} + \frac{1}{4} =$ __________

2. $\frac{3}{6} + \frac{2}{6} =$ __________

3. $\frac{1}{8} + \frac{4}{8} =$ __________ 

Add. Simplify if possible.

4. $\frac{1}{5} + \frac{3}{5} =$ __________

5. $\frac{2}{8} + \frac{3}{8} =$ __________

6. $\frac{1}{3} + \frac{1}{3} =$ __________

7. $\frac{1}{6} + \frac{2}{6} =$ __________

8. $\frac{5}{9} + \frac{1}{9} =$ __________

9. $\frac{2}{7} + \frac{4}{7} =$ __________

Problem Solving

Solve. Simplify if possible.

10. A family went on a long hike. They hiked $\frac{4}{8}$ of the way on the first day and $\frac{3}{8}$ of the way on the second day. What part of the trail did they hike in the two days?

11. On the hike, Derek drank $\frac{2}{6}$ of his water in the morning. He drank $\frac{3}{6}$ of his water in the afternoon. How much of his water did Derek drink?

12. In Kori's class, $\frac{3}{7}$ of her grade is based on test scores and $\frac{3}{7}$ is based on her class participation. How much of her total grade is this?

LESSON 14 — Adding Fractions with Unlike Denominators

Unlike fractions are fractions that have different denominators. Because $\frac{1}{4}$ and $\frac{1}{3}$ have different denominators, they are unlike fractions.

To add fractions, the denominators must be the same. To add unlike fractions, you must first find the common denominator. You must rename the fractions as equivalent fractions so all the fractions have the same denominator. Then you add the numerators. Remember, equivalent fractions are fractions that name the same value.

Example

Add. $\frac{1}{4} + \frac{1}{3} =$ _______

STEP 1 Find a common denominator. Choose the least common multiple (LCM).

Multiples of 4: 4 8 ⑫ 16 20 ...

Multiples of 3: 3 6 9 ⑫ 15 ...

LCM = 12

STEP 2 Rename each fraction using the common denominator.

$$\frac{1}{4} \times \frac{3}{3} = \frac{3}{12}$$

$$\frac{1}{3} \times \frac{4}{4} = \frac{4}{12}$$

STEP 3 Add the like fractions.

$$\frac{3}{12} + \frac{4}{12} = \frac{3+4}{12} = \frac{7}{12}$$

So, $\frac{1}{4} + \frac{1}{3} = \frac{7}{12}$

If your answer is an improper fraction, rewrite it as a mixed or whole number. Remember to simplify your answer if possible.

ON YOUR OWN

Add the unlike fractions.

$$\frac{1}{5} + \frac{1}{2} =$$ _______

Practice

> To add unlike fractions, you must first find the common denominator. Then add only the numerators.

Building Skills

Find the least common denominator.

1. $\frac{3}{4} + \frac{1}{2}$ _________

2. $\frac{1}{3} + \frac{2}{9}$ _________

3. $\frac{1}{4} + \frac{5}{6}$ _________

Add. Rewrite your answer as a mixed or whole number if necessary. Simplify if possible.

4. $\frac{2}{6} + \frac{1}{4} =$ _________

5. $\frac{1}{2} + \frac{3}{8} =$ _________

6. $\frac{2}{5} + \frac{1}{3} =$ _________

7. $\frac{2}{3} + \frac{1}{2} =$ _________

8. $\frac{5}{8} + \frac{3}{4} =$ _________

9. $\frac{5}{6} + \frac{2}{3} =$ _________

Problem Solving

Solve. Simplify if necessary.

10. Carlos practiced pitching for $\frac{1}{3}$ of an hour on Friday and $\frac{1}{2}$ of an hour on Saturday. How long did he practice altogether?

11. Ana spent $\frac{1}{3}$ of an hour cleaning her bike and $\frac{5}{6}$ of an hour riding her bike. How long did she spend with her bike altogether?

12. Terrell spent $\frac{1}{5}$ of his weekly pay on a haircut and $\frac{1}{2}$ on school lunches for the week. What fraction of his weekly pay did Terrell spend?

LESSON 15 Adding Mixed Numbers

When adding mixed numbers, first add the fractions and then add the whole numbers. If the denominators are different, you must find the common denominator. Rewrite the fractions as equivalent fractions. Then add the numerators.

Sometimes the sum in the numerator is greater than the denominator. This means the fraction is greater than 1. Be sure to rename the improper fraction as a mixed number. Simplify the fraction if possible.

Example

Add. $2\frac{1}{2} + 3\frac{3}{4} =$ _________

STEP 1 Rename each fraction using a common denominator.

$$2\frac{1}{2} \longrightarrow 2\frac{2}{4}$$

$$3\frac{3}{4} \longrightarrow 3\frac{3}{4}$$

STEP 2 Add the fractions. Add the whole numbers.

$$2\frac{2}{4} + 3\frac{3}{4} = 5\frac{5}{4}$$

STEP 3 Rename the improper fractions and simplify if necessary.

$$5\frac{5}{4} = 5 + 1\frac{1}{4} = 6\frac{1}{4}$$

So, $2\frac{1}{2} + 3\frac{3}{4} = 6\frac{1}{4}$

ON YOUR OWN

Add the mixed numbers. Simplify if possible.

$$3\frac{5}{8} + 2\frac{1}{8} =$$ _________

Practice

To add mixed numbers, first add the fractions and then the whole numbers.

Building Skills

Add. Rewrite improper fractions if necessary. Simplify if possible.

1. $5\frac{2}{5} + 2\frac{1}{5} =$ _________

2. $6\frac{3}{10} + 2\frac{3}{10} =$ _________

3. $7\frac{1}{4} + 2 =$ _________

4. $2\frac{1}{3} + 1\frac{2}{3} =$ _________

5. $4\frac{4}{5} + 5\frac{1}{2} =$ _________

6. $2\frac{1}{6} + 3\frac{7}{12} =$ _________

7. $1\frac{5}{12} + 6\frac{1}{6} =$ _________

8. $8\frac{2}{9} + 1\frac{1}{3} =$ _________

9. $1\frac{2}{3} + 5\frac{3}{4} + 4\frac{5}{6} =$ _________

Problem Solving

Solve. Rewrite improper fractions if necessary. Simplify if possible.

10. Jessie collected $4\frac{2}{5}$ pounds of aluminum cans for recycling. Alberto collected $5\frac{1}{2}$ pounds. How much did they collect altogether?

11. The first part of a play lasted $1\frac{1}{4}$ hours. The second part of the play lasted $1\frac{1}{3}$ hours. How long was the play?

12. Karla exercised for $15\frac{1}{2}$ minutes on Monday. She exercised for $16\frac{5}{6}$ minutes on Tuesday. How long did she exercise altogether?

Fractions, Decimals, and Percents: Unit 1: Lesson 15
Strengthening Math Skills, SV 9781419039027

Subtracting Fractions with Like Denominators

LESSON 16

Remember, like fractions are fractions that have the same denominator. Because they have the same denominator, $\frac{4}{5}$ and $\frac{3}{5}$ are like fractions. To subtract like fractions, subtract only the numerators.

$$\frac{\text{numerator} - \text{numerator}}{\text{denominator}} \qquad \frac{4}{5} - \frac{3}{5} = \frac{4-3}{5} = \frac{1}{5}$$

To subtract like fractions, subtract the numerators but not the denominators. After you subtract, check that the answer is in the simplest form.

Example

Subtract. $\frac{6}{8} - \frac{2}{8} =$ _________

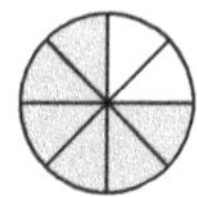 − 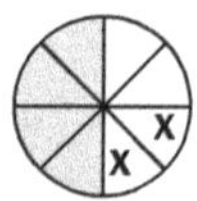 = 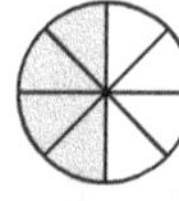

$$\frac{6 \text{ parts shaded}}{8 \text{ total parts}} \quad - \quad \frac{2 \text{ parts shaded}}{8 \text{ total parts}} \quad = \quad \frac{4 \text{ parts shaded}}{8 \text{ total parts}}$$

STEP 1 Subtract the numerators.

$$\frac{6-2}{8} = \frac{4}{8}$$

STEP 2 Reduce to simplest form if possible.

$$\frac{4}{8} = \frac{4 \div 4}{8 \div 4} = \frac{1}{2}$$

So, $\frac{6}{8} - \frac{2}{8} = \frac{1}{2}$

ON YOUR OWN

Pat had $\frac{5}{8}$ of a cup of oil. She used $\frac{3}{8}$ of a cup of oil in a recipe. How much oil does Pat have left? Simplify your answer if possible.

Practice

> To subtract like fractions, subtract only the numerators.

Building Skills

Cross out the correct number of parts. Then solve. Simplify if possible.

1. 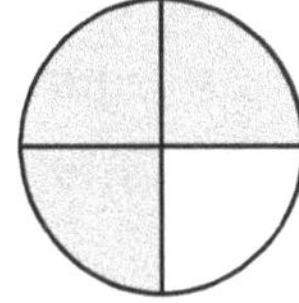

$\dfrac{3}{4} - \dfrac{2}{4} =$ __________

2. 

$\dfrac{5}{6} - \dfrac{1}{6} =$ __________

3. 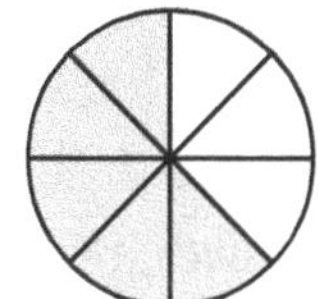

$\dfrac{5}{8} - \dfrac{2}{8} =$ __________

Subtract. Simplify if possible.

4. $\dfrac{6}{7} - \dfrac{3}{7} =$ __________

5. $\dfrac{7}{8} - \dfrac{3}{8} =$ __________

6. $\dfrac{7}{9} - \dfrac{4}{9} =$ __________

7. $\dfrac{4}{5} - \dfrac{1}{5} =$ __________

8. $\dfrac{9}{10} - \dfrac{5}{10} =$ __________

9. $\dfrac{10}{12} - \dfrac{4}{12} =$ __________

Problem Solving

Solve. Simplify if possible.

10. Reggie lives $\dfrac{7}{10}$ of a mile from the mall. Theo lives $\dfrac{4}{10}$ of a mile from the mall. How much farther does Reggie live from the mall than Theo does?

11. One store sells exercise mats that are $\dfrac{7}{8}$ of an inch thick. Another store sells mats that are $\dfrac{5}{8}$ of an inch thick. How much thicker are the mats sold by the first store?

12. A pizza was cut into 8 pieces. Amy ate $\dfrac{3}{8}$ of the pizza. Jarret ate $\dfrac{5}{8}$ of the pizza. How much of the pizza was left?

Subtracting Fractions with Unlike Denominators

LESSON 17

Remember, unlike fractions are fractions that have different denominators. Because $\frac{3}{4}$ and $\frac{3}{5}$ have different denominators, they are unlike fractions.

To subtract fractions, the denominators must be the same. To subtract unlike fractions, you must first find the least common denominator. You must rename the fractions as equivalent fractions so all the fractions have the same denominator. Then you subtract the numerators. Simplify the answer if possible.

Example

Subtract. $\frac{3}{4} - \frac{3}{5} =$ __________

STEP 1 Find a common denominator. Choose the least common multiple.

Multiples of 4: 4 8 12 16 (20) 24 ...

Multiples of 5: 5 10 15 (20) 25 30 ...

LCM = 20

STEP 2 Rename each fraction using the common denominator.

$$\frac{3}{4} \times \frac{5}{5} = \frac{15}{20}$$

$$\frac{3}{5} \times \frac{4}{4} = \frac{12}{20}$$

STEP 3 Subtract the numerators.

$$\frac{15}{20} - \frac{12}{20} = \frac{15 - 12}{20} = \frac{3}{20}$$

So, $\frac{3}{4} - \frac{3}{5} = \frac{3}{20}$

ON YOUR OWN

Subtract the unlike fractions.

$$\frac{4}{5} - \frac{3}{10} =$$ __________

Practice

Building Skills

Subtract the unlike fractions. Simplify if possible.

1. $\dfrac{9}{14} - \dfrac{3}{7} =$ _______________

2. $\dfrac{11}{12} - \dfrac{3}{4} =$ _______________

3. $\dfrac{5}{6} - \dfrac{5}{8} =$ _______________

4. $\dfrac{9}{16} - \dfrac{1}{8} =$ _______________

5. $\dfrac{7}{10} - \dfrac{1}{2} =$ _______________

6. $\dfrac{2}{3} - \dfrac{4}{9} =$ _______________

7. $\dfrac{1}{2} - \dfrac{1}{3} =$ _______________

8. $\dfrac{1}{3} - \dfrac{1}{4} =$ _______________

9. $\dfrac{3}{9} - \dfrac{1}{3} =$ _______________

Problem Solving

Solve. Simplify if possible.

10. Justo ran $\dfrac{9}{10}$ of a mile. Chan ran $\dfrac{3}{4}$ of a mile. How much farther did Justo run than Chan did?

11. Bret did homework for $\dfrac{3}{4}$ of an hour. Bart did homework for $\dfrac{2}{3}$ of an hour. How much longer did Bret do homework than Bart did?

12. Marsha needs $\dfrac{7}{8}$ of a yard of fabric to make a banner. If she has $\dfrac{5}{6}$ of a yard, how much more fabric does she need?

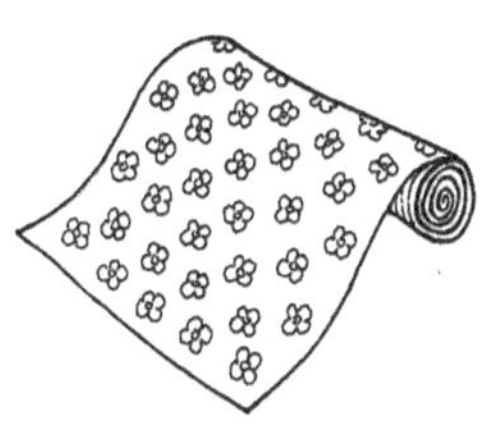

LESSON ⓲ Subtracting Mixed Numbers

When you subtract mixed numbers, be sure to look at the denominators first. If they are not the same, you must find the least common denominator. Subtract the fractions, and then subtract the whole numbers. Reduce to the simplest form.

Sometimes you will need to regroup mixed numbers before you subtract.

Example

Subtract. $2\frac{1}{3} - 1\frac{4}{6} = $ _________

STEP 1 Rename each fraction using a common denominator.

$$2\frac{1}{3} \longrightarrow 2\frac{2}{6}$$
$$-1\frac{4}{6} \longrightarrow 1\frac{4}{6}$$

STEP 2 If necessary, regroup one of the mixed numbers to make an improper fraction.

$$2\frac{1}{3} \longrightarrow 1\frac{8}{6}$$
$$-1\frac{4}{6} \longrightarrow 1\frac{4}{6}$$

STEP 3 Subtract the fractions. Subtract the whole numbers.

$$1\frac{8}{6}$$
$$-1\frac{4}{6}$$
$$\overline{\frac{4}{6}}$$

STEP 4 Reduce to simplest form.

$$\frac{4}{6} = \frac{2}{3} \qquad \text{So, } 2\frac{1}{3} - 1\frac{4}{6} = \frac{2}{3}$$

ON YOUR OWN

Subtract the mixed numbers.

$$3\frac{3}{4} - 1\frac{1}{2} = $$ _________________

Practice

To subtract mixed numbers, make the denominators the same. Subtract the numerators. Then subtract the whole numbers.

Building Skills

Subtract. Regroup if necessary. Simplify if possible.

1. $4\frac{2}{4} - 3\frac{1}{4} =$ _________

2. $8\frac{5}{6} - 1\frac{1}{6} =$ _________

3. $9\frac{8}{12} - \frac{4}{12} =$ _________

4. $3\frac{1}{8} - 2\frac{5}{8} =$ _________

5. $4\frac{1}{4} - 2\frac{3}{4} =$ _________

6. $7 - 5\frac{1}{2} =$ _________

7. $7\frac{4}{9} - 2\frac{1}{3} =$ _________

8. $5\frac{1}{5} - 1\frac{3}{10} =$ _________

9. $5\frac{1}{2} - 2\frac{5}{6} =$ _________

Problem Solving

Solve. Simplify if possible.

10. On Tuesday, Jake and his dog Rocket hiked $2\frac{2}{3}$ miles to the lake. On Wednesday, they hiked $1\frac{1}{3}$ miles to the wildflower center. How much farther did they hike on Tuesday?

11. At the lake, Jake and Rocket did some fishing. Jake used one lure that weighed $2\frac{1}{4}$ ounces. Another lure weighed $1\frac{1}{2}$ ounces. How much more did the first lure weigh?

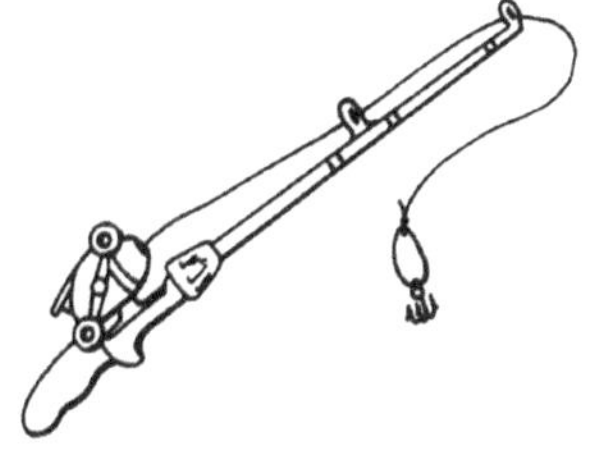

12. Jake caught two fish. One fish weighed 2 pounds. The second fish weighed $2\frac{3}{6}$ pounds. How much more did the second fish weigh?

LESSON 19 · Multiplying a Fraction by a Fraction

To multiply fractions, multiply the numerators and multiply the denominators. Then simplify the answer if possible.

When you multiply two fractions less than 1, the product will be smaller than either of the two fractions.

Example

Multiply. $\frac{1}{2} \times \frac{2}{3} =$ __________ , or $\frac{1}{2}$ of $\frac{2}{3}$

$\frac{2}{3}$

$\frac{1}{2}$ of $\frac{2}{3} = \frac{1}{3}$

STEP 1 Multiply the numerators. Multiply the denominators.

$$\frac{1}{2} \times \frac{2}{3} = \frac{1 \times 2}{2 \times 3} = \frac{2}{6}$$

STEP 2 Reduce to simplest form.

$$\frac{2}{6} = \frac{1}{3}$$

So, $\frac{1}{2} \times \frac{2}{3} = \frac{1}{3}$

ON YOUR OWN

Multiply the fractions.

$$\frac{1}{2} \times \frac{4}{8} =$$

Practice

To multiply fractions, first multiply the numerators. Then multiply the denominators.

Building Skills

Multiply. Simplify if possible.

1. $\frac{1}{4} \times \frac{1}{2} =$ _________

2. $\frac{1}{3} \times \frac{2}{3} =$ _________

3. $\frac{2}{3} \times \frac{1}{5} =$ _________

4. $\frac{3}{4} \times \frac{1}{2} =$ _________

5. $\frac{7}{8} \times \frac{2}{3} =$ _________

6. $\frac{1}{6} \times \frac{3}{4} =$ _________

7. $\frac{1}{5} \times \frac{2}{4} =$ _________

8. $\frac{4}{5} \times \frac{2}{5} =$ _________

9. $\frac{2}{3} \times \frac{5}{7} =$ _________

Problem Solving

Solve. Simplify if possible.

10. Britney's recipe calls for $\frac{4}{5}$ cup of flour. She plans to make $\frac{1}{2}$ of the recipe. How much flour will she use?

11. Mr. Gordon's garden fills $\frac{1}{2}$ of his backyard. He plans to plant flowers in $\frac{1}{3}$ of his garden. How much of the backyard will have flowers?

12. Joe ran $\frac{3}{4}$ of a mile. Juan ran $\frac{2}{3}$ as far as Joe. How far did Juan run?

Multiplying a Fraction by a Whole Number

LESSON 20

To multiply a fraction by a whole number, you must rename the whole number as an improper fraction. The improper fraction will have a denominator of 1. Then multiply the new numerators and denominators. Simplify the answer if possible.

Example

Multiply. $\frac{2}{5} \times 10 =$ _____________

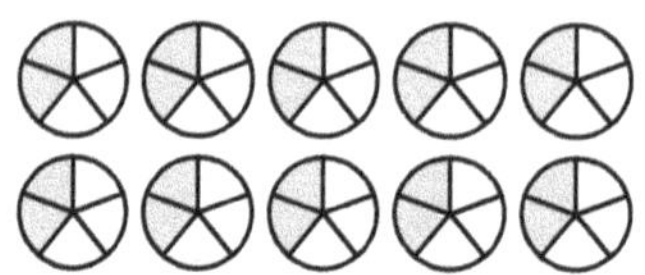

$\frac{20}{5}$ in all.

$\frac{20}{5} = 4$

STEP 1 Rename the whole number as an improper fraction.

$$10 = \frac{10}{1}$$

STEP 2 Multiply the numerators. Multiply the denominators.

$$\frac{2}{5} \times \frac{10}{1} = \frac{2 \times 10}{5 \times 1} = \frac{20}{5}$$

STEP 3 Reduce to simplest form.

$$\frac{20}{5} = 4$$

So, $\frac{2}{5} \times 10 = 4$

ON YOUR OWN

Multiply the fraction by the whole number.

$$\frac{1}{2} \times 8 =$$

Practice

Building Skills

Multiply. Simplify if possible.

To multiply a fraction by a whole number, first change the whole number to an improper fraction.

1. $\frac{1}{4} \times 16 =$ _________

2. $\frac{1}{3} \times 12 =$ _________

3. $\frac{1}{7} \times 21 =$ _________

4. $\frac{3}{4} \times 6 =$ _________

5. $\frac{3}{5} \times 7 =$ _________

6. $15 \times \frac{2}{3} =$ _________

7. $6 \times \frac{4}{5} =$ _________

8. $\frac{3}{8} \times 11 =$ _________

9. $\frac{5}{6} \times 5 =$ _________

Problem Solving

Solve. Simplify if possible.

10. Mia has 9 sheets of paper. She gives $\frac{1}{3}$ of her paper to Keena. How many sheets of paper does Mia give to Keena?

11. Monique is making 20 ribbons for the spring dance. Each ribbon is $\frac{3}{4}$ yard long. How many yards of material will she need?

12. Kristi had 24 eggs. She used $\frac{2}{3}$ of her eggs in recipes. How many eggs did she use in recipes?

Fractions, Decimals, and Percents: Unit 1: Lesson 20
Strengthening Math Skills, SV 9781419039027

LESSON 21 — Multiplying a Fraction by a Mixed Number

You can multiply a fraction by a mixed number in different ways. One of the easiest ways is to change the mixed number to an improper fraction.

Example

Multiply. $\frac{1}{2} \times 1\frac{3}{4} =$ __________

STEP 1 Rename the mixed number as an improper fraction.

$$1\frac{3}{4} = \frac{7}{4}$$

STEP 2 Multiply the numerators. Multiply the denominators.

$$\frac{1}{2} \times \frac{7}{4} = \frac{1 \times 7}{2 \times 4} = \frac{7}{8}$$

STEP 3 Reduce to simplest form if possible.

$\frac{7}{8}$ is in simplest form.

So, $\frac{1}{2} \times 1\frac{3}{4} = \frac{7}{8}$

ON YOUR OWN

Multiply the fraction by the mixed number.

$$\frac{1}{3} \times 2\frac{1}{4} = \text{\_\_\_\_\_\_\_}$$

Practice

> To multiply a fraction by a mixed number, first change the mixed number to an improper fraction.

Building Skills

Multiply. Simplify if possible.

1. $\frac{1}{3} \times 3\frac{1}{5} =$ _________

2. $\frac{1}{6} \times 4\frac{1}{2} =$ _________

3. $\frac{1}{2} \times 3\frac{1}{3} =$ _________

4. $\frac{1}{3} \times 3\frac{1}{2} =$ _________

5. $\frac{1}{4} \times 2\frac{5}{6} =$ _________

6. $\frac{2}{3} \times 1\frac{4}{5} =$ _________

7. $\frac{3}{4} \times 1\frac{2}{3} =$ _________

8. $2\frac{1}{2} \times \frac{2}{5} =$ _________

9. $\frac{5}{6} \times 5\frac{3}{5} =$ _________

Problem Solving

Solve. Simplify if possible.

10. Angela hiked $\frac{3}{4}$ of a mile. Pedro hiked $1\frac{1}{2}$ times farther than Angela. How far did Pedro hike?

11. Sydney has $\frac{4}{5}$ of a cup of bubble soap. Meela has $2\frac{1}{4}$ times more bubble soap than Sydney. How many cups of bubble soap does Meela have?

12. A formula uses $\frac{2}{3}$ of a cup of water. Roslyn wants to make $2\frac{1}{2}$ times the formula. How many cups of water will she need?

LESSON 22 Dividing Fractions

To divide fractions, you must use the **reciprocal** of the divisor. The reciprocal is made by changing the places of the numerator and denominator.

The product of a number and its reciprocal is 1. For example, the reciprocal of $\frac{2}{3}$ is $\frac{3}{2}$. If you multiply $\frac{2}{3}$ by $\frac{3}{2}$, the product is 1.

$$\frac{2}{3} \times \frac{3}{2} = \frac{6}{6} = 1$$

To divide fractions, write a multiplication sentence using the dividend and the reciprocal of the divisor. Reduce to simplest form if possible.

Example

Divide. $\frac{1}{2} \div \frac{1}{3} =$ _________

STEP 1 Write the reciprocal of the divisor. The divisor is the second fraction in the division sentence.

The reciprocal of $\frac{1}{3}$ is $\frac{3}{1}$.

STEP 2 Use the reciprocal to write a multiplication sentence.

$$\frac{1}{2} \times \frac{3}{1} = \frac{1 \times 3}{2 \times 1} = \frac{3}{2}$$

STEP 3 Reduce to simplest form if possible.

$$\frac{3}{2} = 1\frac{1}{2}$$

So, $\frac{1}{2} \div \frac{1}{3} = 1\frac{1}{2}$

ON YOUR OWN

Divide the fractions.

$$\frac{2}{3} \div \frac{1}{3} =$$ _________

Fractions, Decimals, and Percents: Unit 1: Lesson 22
Strengthening Math Skills, SV 9781419039027

Practice

To divide by
a fraction, multiply
by the reciprocal of
the divisor.

Building Skills

Write the reciprocal number.

1. $\frac{1}{4}$ __________

2. $\frac{3}{8}$ __________

3. $\frac{5}{2}$ __________

Divide. Simplify if possible.

4. $\frac{2}{4} \div \frac{1}{8} =$ __________

5. $\frac{1}{3} \div \frac{2}{5} =$ __________

6. $\frac{3}{4} \div \frac{1}{2} =$ __________

7. $\frac{3}{5} \div \frac{1}{5} =$ __________

8. $\frac{2}{3} \div \frac{2}{3} =$ __________

9. $\frac{7}{10} \div 2 =$ __________

Problem Solving

Solve. Simplify if possible.

10. Chad is making party invitations. Each invitation takes $\frac{1}{8}$ sheet of paper. Chad has $\frac{3}{4}$ of a sheet of paper. How many invitations can he make?

11. Leela has $\frac{3}{4}$ cup of nuts for cookies. She must use $\frac{1}{3}$ cup of nuts for each dozen cookies. How many dozen cookies can she make?

12. How many pieces of rope $\frac{1}{6}$ yard long can you cut from a piece of rope that is $\frac{2}{3}$ yard long?

LESSON ㉓ Fractions and Time

You can use fractions to tell about time. You know there are 60 minutes in 1 hour.

$\frac{1}{4}$ hour = 15 minutes

$\frac{1}{4} \times 60 = \frac{1}{4} \times \frac{60}{1} = \frac{60}{4} = 15$

$\frac{1}{2}$ hour = 30 minutes

$\frac{1}{2} \times 60 = \frac{1}{2} \times \frac{60}{1} = \frac{60}{2} = 30$

$\frac{3}{4}$ hour = 45 minutes

$\frac{3}{4} \times 60 = \frac{3}{4} \times \frac{60}{1} = \frac{180}{4} = 45$

1 hour = 60 minutes

Example

Write the time that has passed as a fraction.

Lin started reading her book at 6:00. She stopped reading at 6:30. How long did she read her book?

STEP 1 Find how many minutes have passed.

From 6:00 to 6:30 = 30 minutes

6:30 − 6:00 = 0:30

STEP 2 Find what fraction of an hour has passed.

$$\frac{30 \text{ minutes}}{60 \text{ minutes}} = \frac{30}{60} = \frac{1}{2} \text{ hour}$$

So, Lin read her book for $\frac{1}{2}$ hour.

Practice

> An hour has 4 quarters. Each quarter is 15 minutes long.

Building Skills

Write the time that has passed as a fraction.

1. 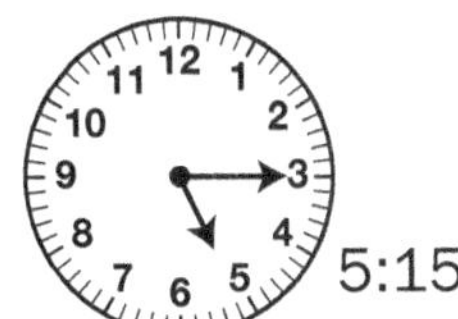 5:15   5:45   Time passed = ___________ hour

2.  4:00   4:45   Time passed = ___________ hour

Write the time that has passed as a mixed number.

3. 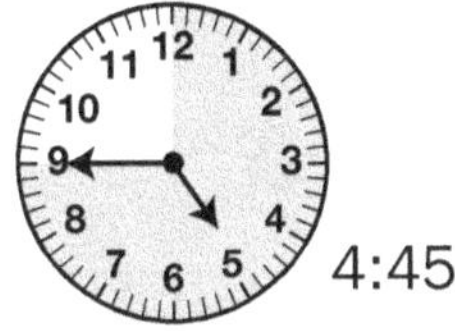 3:00   4:30   Time passed = ___________ hours

4.  12:30   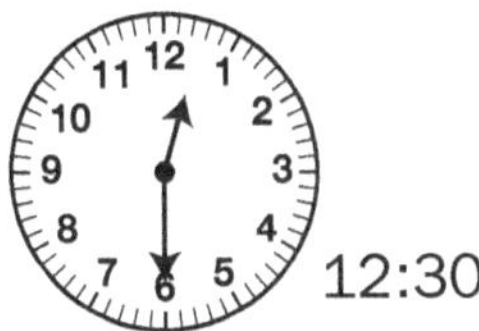 1:45   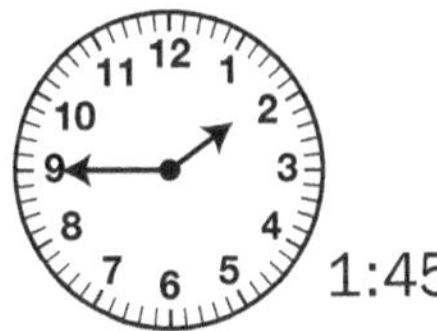 Time passed = ___________ hours

Problem Solving

Solve.

5. Teena and Lena talked on the phone from 7:45 to 8:00. What part of an hour did they talk? Write your answer as a fraction.

6. Sandi went to a movie. The movie started at 7:15 and ended at 9:00. How many hours did the movie last? Write your answer as a mixed number.

7. One third of an hour is 20 minutes. How many minutes is two thirds of an hour?

8. Jerrett had a soccer game at 2:30. The game lasted $2\frac{1}{2}$ hours. At what time did the game end?

LESSON 24 Fractions and Measurement

A customary ruler breaks inches into fractions of an inch. Many rulers show lengths as small as $\frac{1}{8}$ or $\frac{1}{16}$ of an inch.

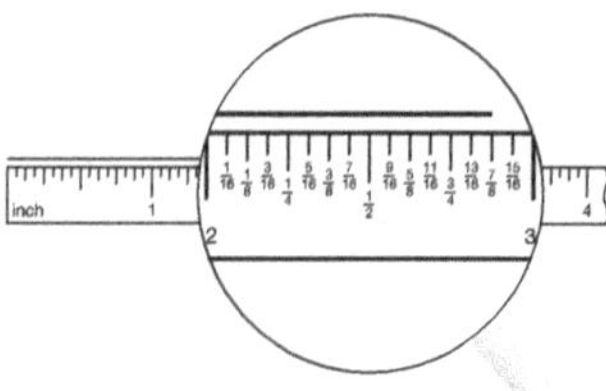

This is a section of a customary ruler. This ruler breaks inches into halves, quarters, eighths, and sixteenths. Sometimes you must measure very carefully, so you may need to use eighths or sixteenths.

Example

Use a customary ruler. Measure the line segment to the part of an inch that gives the most precise measurement.

STEP 1 Set the left end of the ruler at the beginning of the line segment. Notice where the end of the line stops on the ruler.

STEP 2 First count the number of inches.

The line is over 3 inches long.

STEP 3 Then count the fractions of an inch.

The line is shorter than $3\frac{1}{2}$ inches but longer than $3\frac{1}{4}$ inches. The end of the line is on an eighth of an inch mark. Count the number of eighths. The line ends at $\frac{3}{8}$.

So, the line is $3\frac{3}{8}$ inches long.

ON YOUR OWN

Use a customary ruler. Measure the line segment to the part of an inch that gives the most precise measurement.

Practice

> Be sure to line up your ruler carefully with what you are measuring.

Building Skills

Use a customary ruler. Measure the line segment to the part of an inch that gives the most precise measurement.

1. ________________________   ___________

2. ____________________________   ___________

3. ____   ___________

Use a customary ruler. Draw a line to the given length.

4. $2\frac{1}{4}$ inches •

5. $3\frac{3}{8}$ inches •

6. $2\frac{15}{16}$ inches •

Problem Solving

Solve.

7. Eric made the chart below to keep track of how much wood he had for projects. He forgot to enter some of the numbers. Complete the chart.

Type of Wood	Start With	Feet Used	Feet Left
Oak	$15\frac{1}{2}$	$9\frac{1}{4}$	
Pine	$22\frac{5}{8}$		$10\frac{1}{4}$
Maple		$12\frac{3}{4}$	$2\frac{1}{6}$

8. Eric decided to make a small box out of pine. He started with $10\frac{1}{4}$ feet. He used $3\frac{3}{4}$ feet to make the box. How much pine did he have left?

LESSON **25** Probability

Probability is the chance that an event will happen. The outcome is the result of the event. Probability can be written as a fraction.

$$\frac{\text{number of a kind of item or event}}{\text{total number of items or events}}$$

Example

What is the probability the spinner will stop on a square?

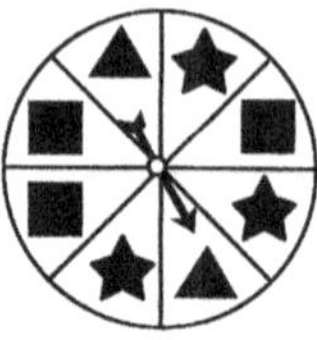

STEP 1 Read the problem carefully. What does the question ask?

The question asks what the chances are that the spinner will stop on a square.

STEP 2 Count the number of squares on the spinner.

There are 3 squares. This number goes on the top of the probability fraction.

STEP 3 The spinner can stop on any section. Count the total number of sections on the spinner.

There are 8 sections on the spinner. This number goes on the bottom of the probability fraction.

$\frac{3}{8}$ ⟵ number of squares
⟵ total number of sections

So, the probability of the spinner stopping on a square is 3 out of 8 or $\frac{3}{8}$.

ON YOUR OWN

What is the probability the spinner will stop on a triangle?
Write your answer as a fraction.

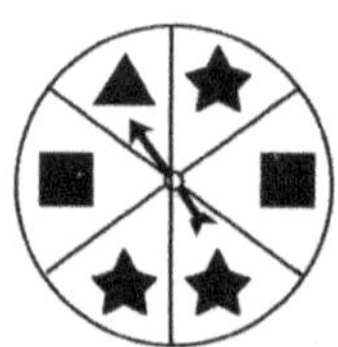

Practice

Probability names the number of chances in the total number of opportunities.

Building Skills

For problems 1–4, use the top spinner. Name the probability of spinning each color. Write your answer as a fraction in simplest form.

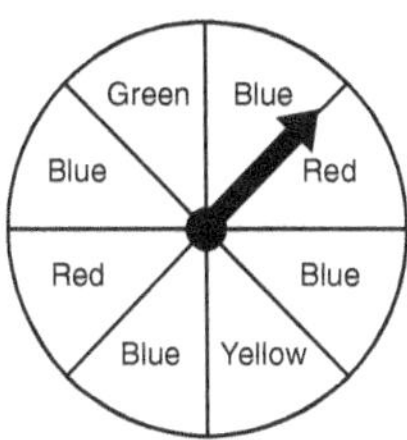

1. red __________

2. blue __________

3. green __________

4. yellow __________

For problems 5–8, use the bottom spinner. Name the probability of spinning each number. Write your answer as a fraction in simplest form.

5. 1 __________

6. 3 __________

7. 4 __________

8. 5 __________

Problem Solving

Solve. Write your answer as a fraction. Simplify if possible.

9. A bag contained 5 red marbles, 3 blue marbles, 2 green marbles, and 1 yellow marble. Ryan picked a marble from the bag. What is the probability Ryan picked a green marble?

10. A bag contained 3 red marbles, 6 blue marbles, 3 green marbles, and 3 yellow marbles. Jessica picked a marble from the bag. What is the probability Jessica picked a blue marble?

LESSON 26   Ratios

A **ratio** compares two numbers or amounts. A ratio may compare a part to the whole or the whole to a part. It may also compare a part to another part. Like fractions, ratios should be written in simplest form.

A ratio can be written as a fraction ($\frac{1}{2}$), with a colon (1:2), or in words (1 to 2).

For example, four cars and two trucks are parked in a parking lot. The ratio of cars to trucks is 4 to 2. This ratio can also be written as 4:2 or $\frac{4}{2}$. In simplest form, the ratio is $\frac{2}{1}$.

Example

What is the ratio of shaded parts to total parts?

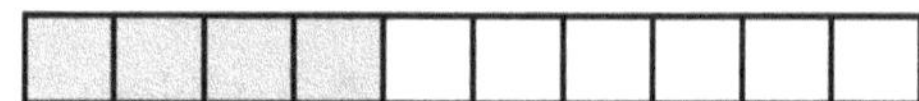

STEP 1 This problem compares parts to the whole. First count the number of shaded parts.

There are 4 shaded parts. This number will go first in a ratio or on the top of a ratio fraction.

STEP 2 Next count the total parts.

There are 10 total parts. This number will go second in a ratio or on the bottom of a ratio fraction.

STEP 3 Write the ratio.

The ratio of parts to whole is 4 to 10.

The ratio can be written as 4 to 10, 4:10, or $\frac{4}{10}$.
In simplest form, the ratio is $\frac{2}{5}$.

ON YOUR OWN

What is the ratio of shaded parts to total parts? Write your answer as a fraction in simplest form.

Practice

A ratio can be written three ways: as a fraction, with a colon, or in words.

Building Skills

What is the ratio of shaded parts to total parts? Write your answer as a fraction in simplest form.

1. ___________

2. ___________

Write each ratio as a fraction in simplest form.

3. 4 to 5 _________

4. 2:3 _________

5. 6 to 8 _________

6. 10:25 _________

7. 5 to 10 _________

8. 4 to 12 _________

Problem Solving

Solve. Write your answer as a fraction. Simplify if possible.

9. There are 20 students in the school play. Eight of the students are boys. The rest are girls. What is the ratio of boys to girls in the play?

10. There are 12 apples in a basket. Four of the apples are green. What is the ratio of green apples to the total number of apples in the basket?

LESSON 27 — What Is a Decimal?

A **decimal** is a number that uses place value and a **decimal point (.)** to show a value less than 1, such as tenths or hundredths. The numbers to the left of the decimal point are whole numbers. The numbers to the right of the decimal point represent some part of 1. Like fractions, decimals show parts of a whole. So, the decimal 2.5 is the same as the mixed number $2\frac{5}{10}$.

Decimals can be written using numbers or words. When a whole number is followed by a decimal part, the decimal part is read as *and*.

1.7 = one and seven tenths

Example

Write the decimal and the decimal name shown by the shaded part of the figure.

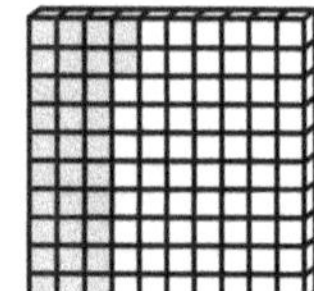

STEP 1 Count the number of blocks in the whole shape.

In this shape, there are 100 blocks.

STEP 2 Count the number of blocks that are shaded.

There are 32 blocks that are shaded. So, 32 of 100 blocks are shaded. If the 100 blocks represent 1, then the 32 shaded blocks represent a value less than 1.

STEP 3 Write the number of shaded blocks as a decimal. If there is no whole number in the ones place, write a 0 (zero) there.

If the 100 blocks = 1, then the 32 blocks = 0.32.

STEP 4 Write the decimal as words.

0.32 = 32 hundredths

ON YOUR OWN

Write the decimal and the decimal name shown by the shaded part of the figure.

Practice

Building Skills

Write the decimal and the decimal name shown by the shaded part of each figure.

The numbers to the left of the decimal point are greater than 1. The numbers to the right of the decimal point are less than 1.

1.  _______________

____

2. 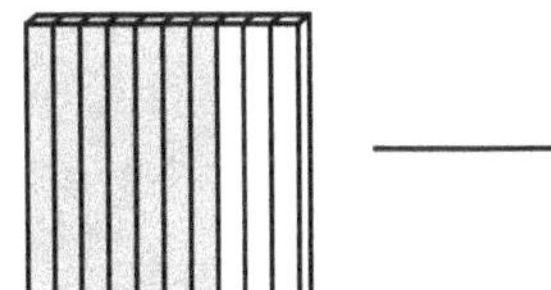 _______________

____

3. 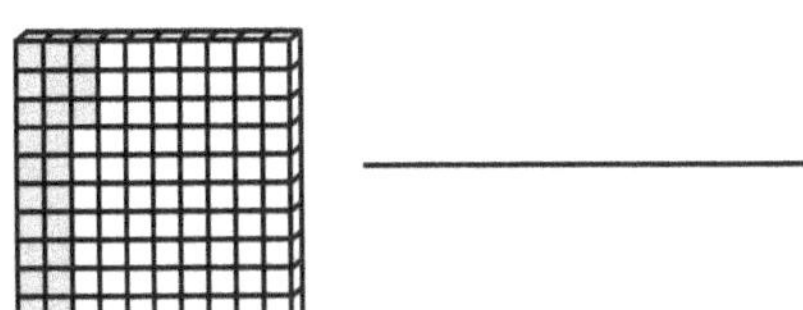 _______________

____

4. 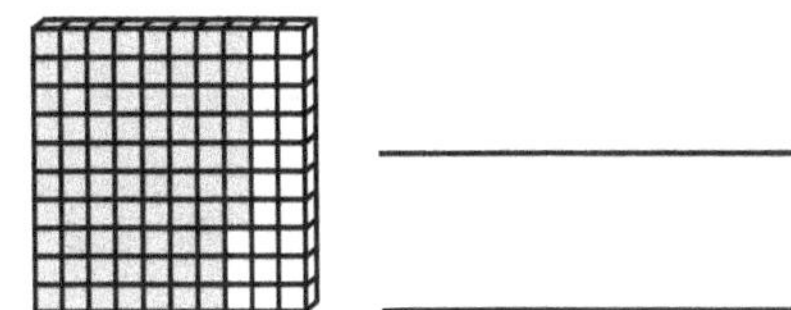 _______________

____

Shade the model to show the decimal.

5. 0.9

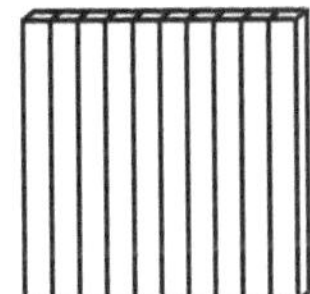

6. 0.30

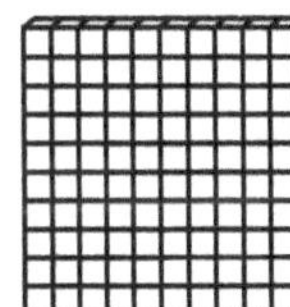

Problem Solving

Solve.

7. Teera had 100 spaces in her coin collection book. She had coins in 71 spaces. Write a decimal to show the part of the book that had coins. Then name the decimal in words.

LESSON 28   Place Value

Decimals use the place-value system.

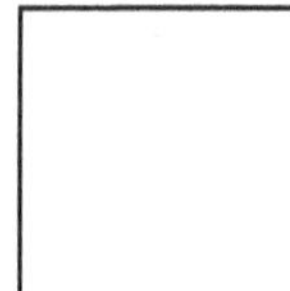 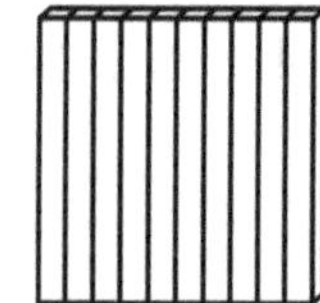 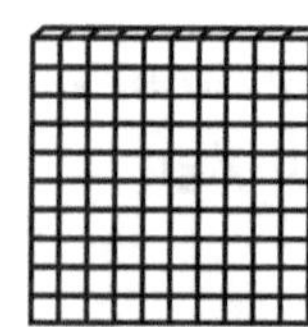

This square represents one whole, or 1.

The whole is divided into 10 equal parts. Each part is $\frac{1}{10}$ of the whole, or 0.1.

The whole is divided into 100 equal parts. Each part is $\frac{1}{100}$ of the whole, or 0.01.

You can use a place-value chart to find the value of each digit in a decimal.

Example

The number 43.21 is a decimal in standard form. Write the decimal in the place-value chart. Then write the decimal in a number sentence and in word form.

STEP 1 First find the decimal point in the number. Then find the decimal point in the chart. Write the digits in the correct columns in the chart.

Tens	Ones	Decimal point	Tenths	Hundredths
4	3	. (and)	2	1

STEP 2 Use the place-value chart to write the decimal as a number sentence.

43.21 = 4 tens + 3 ones + 2 tenths + 1 hundredth

STEP 3 Write the number sentence in word form.

4 tens + 3 ones + 2 tenths + 1 hundredth = forty-three and twenty-one hundredths

ON YOUR OWN

Write the number 15.67 in the place-value chart. Then write the number as a number sentence and in word form.

Tens	Ones	Decimal point	Tenths	Hundredths
		. (and)		

Practice

> Use a place-value chart to help you work with decimals.

Building Skills

Write each number in the place-value chart. Then write the number as a number sentence and in word form.

1. 7.3

Tens	Ones	Decimal point	Tenths	Hundredths
		. (and)		

____

2. 47.17

Tens	Ones	Decimal point	Tenths	Hundredths
		. (and)		

____

Write each word form as a number in the place-value chart.

3. thirteen and twenty-three hundredths

Tens	Ones	Decimal point	Tenths	Hundredths
		. (and)		

4. ninety-five and six tenths

Tens	Ones	Decimal point	Tenths	Hundredths
		. (and)		

Problem Solving

For each problem, write the decimal as a number in standard form.

5. Ling lives 3 and 5 tenths miles from the school.

____

6. A marathon is 26 and 3 tenths miles long.

____

7. A bottle of ink contains 2 and 6 tenths ounces.

____

8. Dara bought a sack of oranges that weighed 5 and 25 hundredths pounds.

____

LESSON 29 Changing Fractions to Decimals

Do you remember ratios? A ratio is often written as a fraction. Sometimes you want to express the ratio as a decimal. Changing a proper fraction to a decimal is easy. Suppose that 9 of 10 people in your class are right-handed. You can write that ratio as $\frac{9}{10}$. You can also write it as 0.9.

Example

Change $\frac{4}{5}$ to a decimal.

STEP 1 Find an equivalent fraction with a denominator of 10 or 100. To find an equivalent fraction, multiply the numerator and the denominator by the same number.

$$\frac{4}{5} \times \frac{2}{2} = \frac{8}{10}$$

STEP 2 Write the name of the equivalent fraction. Then write the decimal.

$$\frac{8}{10} \longrightarrow \text{eight tenths} \longrightarrow 0.8$$

So, the fraction $\frac{4}{5}$ can be written as the decimal 0.8.

Bonus Tip

There's a really easy way to change a proper fraction to a decimal. First divide the numerator by the denominator. Then put a decimal point before the quotient. Try it.

$$4 \div 5 = 0.80$$

Remember, if you change a proper fraction to a decimal, the answer will always be less than 1.

ON YOUR OWN

Change $\frac{1}{2}$ to a decimal. Use the regular method and the bonus method. Show your work.

Practice

Building Skills

Complete the table with the decimal and words for each fraction.

To change proper fractions to decimals quickly, divide the numerator by the denominator and put a decimal point before the answer.

	Fraction	Decimal	Words
1.	$\frac{3}{10}$		
2.	$\frac{17}{100}$		
3.	$\frac{2}{5}$		
4.	$\frac{3}{4}$		
5.	$\frac{11}{20}$		

Problem Solving

Solve. You may use any method to change the fraction to a decimal. Show your work. Remember to write a 0 in the ones place.

6. Dudley took a math test. Dudley thought $\frac{9}{10}$ of the problems were really hard. Write this fraction as a decimal.

7. Kurt received $\frac{7}{20}$ of the votes in the election for club president. Write this fraction as a decimal.

8. Mr. Oliver did not like junk mail. Three out of 5 pieces of mail he received were junk. Write this ratio as a decimal.

Fractions, Decimals, and Percents: Unit 2: Lesson 29
Strengthening Math Skills, SV 9781419039027

LESSON ③⓪ Rounding Decimals

Sometimes you will need to round decimals to estimate. Rounding decimals is similar to rounding whole numbers.

To round a decimal to the nearest whole number, look at the digit in the tenths place. If the digit is 5 or greater, add 1 to the digit in the ones place and drop the other digits to the right of the decimal point. If the digit is less than 5, drop all the digits to the right of the decimal point.

$$7.8 = 8$$
$$5.2 = 5$$

To round a decimal to the nearest whole tenth, look at the digit in the hundredths place. If the digit is 5 or greater, add 1 to the digit in the tenths place and drop the other digits to the right of the decimal point. If the digit is less than 5, drop all the digits to the right of the tenths place.

$$3.37 = 3.4$$
$$6.23 = 6.2$$

Example

Round 4.58 to the nearest tenth.

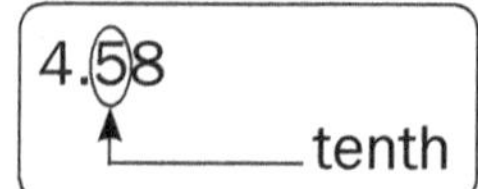

STEP 1 Find the digit in the place value you want to round to and circle.

STEP 2 Underline the digit to the right of the circled digit.

STEP 3 If the underlined digit is 5 or greater, add 1 to the circled digit. If the underlined digit is less than 5, do not change the circled digit. Drop the remaining numbers to the right of the circled number.

8 > 5 Because 8 is greater than 5, add 1 to the circled digit. Then drop the 8.

So, when rounded to the nearest tenth, 4.58 is 4.6.

ON YOUR OWN

Round 3.53 to the nearest tenth.

Practice

Building Skills

> A decimal is rounded up or down based on the number to the right of the place you want to round to.

Round each decimal to the nearest whole number.

1. 6.9 __________   **2.** 3.3 __________   **3.** 1.7 __________

4. 2.5 __________   **5.** 1.2 __________   **6.** 5.4 __________

Round each decimal to the nearest tenth.

7. 8.88 __________   **8.** 1.37 __________   **9.** 3.93 __________

10. 2.75 __________   **11.** 7.45 __________   **12.** 4.09 __________

Problem Solving

Use rounding to solve each problem.

13. Katy rounded a decimal to the nearest tenth. Her answer was 24.5. Which decimal did she round? Circle your answer.

24.37   24.58   24.51   24.85

14. A lizard is 6.5 inches long. What is the length of the lizard to the nearest whole number?

15. A pencil is 5.45 inches long. What is the length of the pencil to the nearest tenth?

Fractions, Decimals, and Percents: Unit 2: Lesson 30
Strengthening Math Skills SV 9781419039027

LESSON 31 Comparing Decimals

To compare two decimals, line up the decimal points. Beginning at the left, compare the value of the digits in each place. The greater number is the one with the greater digit farthest to the left. You can use a place-value chart to help you compare decimals.

Use the symbol < to mean "is less than."   3.3 < 3.5
Use the symbol > to mean "is greater than."   2.7 > 2.4
Use the symbol = to mean "equals."   5.5 = 5.50

Sometimes you will have decimals with a different number of places to the right of the decimal points. You can add a 0 to the end of a decimal without changing its value.

Example

Compare 27.73 and 27.82. Use <, >, or =.

STEP 1 Write the numbers in the place-value chart.

Tens	Ones	Decimal point	Tenths	Hundredths
2	7	.	7	3
2	7	.	8	2

same number same number   7 and 8 are
of tens   of ones   different

STEP 2 Compare digits. Start on the left. When you find two different digits in the same place, underline them.

27.7̲3   27.8̲2

STEP 3 Compare the underlined digits. The number with the greater underlined digit is the greater number.

7 < 8, so 27.73 < 27.82

ON YOUR OWN

Compare 9.91 and 9.90. Use <, >, or =. Draw a place-value chart if you need help.

Practice

Building Skills

Compare the decimals. Write <, >, or =.

To compare decimals, line up the decimal points. Beginning at the left, compare the value of the digits in each place.

1. 1.8 $\bigcirc$ 1.5

2. 3.3 $\bigcirc$ 3.30

3. 4.51 $\bigcirc$ 4.5

4. 13.45 $\bigcirc$ 13.54

5. 21.01 $\bigcirc$ 21.10

6. 55.55 $\bigcirc$ 55.56

7. 6.8 $\bigcirc$ 6.76

8. 11.12 $\bigcirc$ 11.21

Problem Solving

Solve.

9. A red jar holds 1.75 pints of liquid. A blue jar holds 1.7 pints of liquid. Which jar holds more liquid?

10. In June, it rained 0.20 inch in Phoenix. In Tucson, it rained 0.17 inch. In Scottsdale, it rained 0.27 inch. Which city had the least rainfall?

LESSON 32   Adding Decimals

Add decimals in the same way you add whole numbers. First write the numbers so the decimal points line up. Check to see if there are empty spaces to the right of the last digit of any number. If there are, add zeros as placeholders. You can use a place-value chart to help you add.

Example

Add. 3.5 + 1.62 = __________

STEP 1 Write the decimals in the place-value chart so the decimal points line up.

		Ones	Decimal point	Tenths	Hundredths
		3	.	5	0
	+	1	.	6	2
			.		

STEP 2 Add zeros as placeholders, if necessary.
Add a 0 after 3.5.

STEP 3 Put a decimal point in the answer directly under the other decimal points.

STEP 4 Add. Regroup if necessary.

$$
\begin{array}{r}
1\\
3.5\,0\\
+\ 1.6\,2\\
\hline
5.1\,2
\end{array}
$$

When you add the tenths place, you must regroup. Move 1 to the ones place.

So, 3.5 + 1.62 = 5.12

ON YOUR OWN

Add. Draw a place-value chart if you need help.

$$0.4 + 1.5 = \underline{\hspace{2cm}}$$

Practice

To add decimals, be sure to line up the decimal points. Then add the decimals as you would whole numbers.

Building Skills

Find each sum. Use the place-value chart to help you.

	Ones	Decimal point	Tenths	Hundredths
		.		
		.		
		.		

1. $0.3 + 0.6 =$ _______

2. $0.9 + 0.4 =$ _______

3. $1.44 + 1.7 =$ _______

Find the sum.

4.   0.6
   + 0.8

5.   0.7 3
   + 0.5 2

6.   0.8 1
   + 0.3 9

7.   1.5
   + 0.8 5

8.   6.6 7
   + 4.1 2

9.   9.7 5
   + 2.8 6

Problem Solving

Solve.

10. Travis likes to run. One day he ran 1.25 miles. The next day he ran 2.75 miles. How many miles did he run on the two days?

11. Leela poured 3.7 quarts of water in a large tub. Then she added 4.45 quarts more. How much water did she pour in the tub?

12. Ms. Romero bought 8.85 yards of fabric to make curtains. Then she bought 5.25 yards of fabric to make throw pillows. How much fabric did she buy in all?

Fractions, Decimals, and Percents: Unit 2: Lesson 32
Strengthening Math Skills, SV 9781419039027

Name _______________________ Date _______________________

LESSON 33 Subtracting Decimals

Subtract decimals in the same way you subtract whole numbers. First write the numbers so the decimal points line up. Check to see if there are empty spaces to the right of the last digit of any number. If there are, add zeros as placeholders. You can use a place-value chart to help you subtract.

Subtract. 1.7 – 0.51 = _______

STEP 1 Write the decimals in the place-value chart so the decimal points line up.

	Ones		Tenths	Hundredths
	1	.	7	0
–	0	.	5	1
		.		

STEP 2 Add zeros as placeholders, if necessary.

Add a 0 after 1.7.

STEP 3 Put a decimal point in the answer directly under the other decimal points.

STEP 4 Subtract. Regroup if necessary.

$$\begin{array}{r} \overset{6\ 10}{1.\cancel{7}0} \\ -\ 0.5\,1 \\ \hline 1.1\,9 \end{array}$$

When you subtract 1 from 0, you must regroup.

So, 1.7 – 0.51 = 1.19

ON YOUR OWN

Subtract. Draw a place-value chart if you need help.

3.6 – 1.5 = _______

Fractions, Decimals, and Perce
Strengthening M

Practice

Building Skills

Find each difference. Use the place-value chart to help you.

		Ones	Decimal point	Tenths	Hundredths
			.		
			.		
			.		

1. $0.9 - 0.3 =$ _______ **2.** $0.63 - 0.49 =$ _______ **3.** $2.5 - 1.77 =$ _______

Find the difference.

4.
$$0.2\,6$$
$$-\ 0.1\,8$$

5.
$$2.8$$
$$-\ 1.7\,6$$

6.
$$0.7\,1$$
$$-\ 0.2\,9$$

7.
$$4.5$$
$$-\ 1.4\,9$$

8.
$$1\,2.5\,7$$
$$-\ 6.3\,2$$

9.
$$9.7\,5$$
$$-\ 7.5$$

Problem Solving

Solve.

10. The painter had 5.5 gallons of paint to begin a job. She used 1.75 gallons to paint one room. How much paint did she have left?

11. The carpenter had a board that was 1.9 meters long. He cut off a piece that was 0.66 meter long. How much of the board did he have left?

12. The plumbers think they need 22.25 ounces of glue for a job. They have 13.75 ounces of glue. How much more glue do they need?

Multiplying Decimals by Whole Numbers

LESSON 34

Multiply decimals by whole numbers in the same way you multiply whole numbers. You do not need to line up the decimal points. Just find the product. Then count the number of decimal places in the factors. Write the decimal point in the product that many places from the right.

Example

Multiply. $23.45 \times 6 =$ _____________

STEP 1 Multiply. Ignore the decimal point for now.

$$\begin{array}{r} {}^{2}\ {}^{2}\ {}^{3} \\ 23.45 \\ \times\qquad 6 \\ \hline 14070 \end{array}$$

STEP 2 Count the number of decimal places in both factors.

23.45 ⟵—— There are 2 decimal places in this factor.
$\times\quad 6$ ⟵—— There are 0 decimal places in this factor.
14070 ⟶ There is a total of 2 decimal places in the two factors.

STEP 3 Start at the right side of the product. Count 2 places to the left and write the decimal point there.

$$\begin{array}{r} 23.45 \\ \times\qquad 6 \\ \hline 140.70 \end{array}$$ ⟵—— Put 2 decimal places in the product.

So, $23.45 \times 6 = 140.70$

ON YOUR OWN

Multiply. Show your work.

$$5.6 \times 3 =$$ _____________

Name _______________________________________ Date _____________________________

Practice

Building Skills

Write the decimal point in each product.

1. $0.19 \times 4 = 0\,7\,6$

2. $12.66 \times 2 = 2\,5\,3\,2$

3. $7 \times 1.23 = 8\,6\,1$

4. $5.42 \times 5 = 2\,7\,1\,0$

Find the product.

5.
$$\begin{array}{r} 4.11 \\ \times\ \ \ 5 \\ \hline \end{array}$$

6.
$$\begin{array}{r} 0.22 \\ \times\ \ \ 3 \\ \hline \end{array}$$

7.
$$\begin{array}{r} 10 \\ \times\ 0.6 \\ \hline \end{array}$$

8.
$$\begin{array}{r} 0.5 \\ \times\ 8 \\ \hline \end{array}$$

9.
$$\begin{array}{r} 9.99 \\ \times\ \ \ 2 \\ \hline \end{array}$$

10.
$$\begin{array}{r} 25 \\ \times\ 0.2 \\ \hline \end{array}$$

Problem Solving

Solve.

11. At the store, 3 clerks work 6.5 hours each day. What is the total number of hours the 3 clerks work?

12. Barry and Barbie are making 5 banners for the school banquet. They need 3.25 yards of material for each banner. How much material will they need?

Fractions, Decimals, and Percents: Unit 2: Lesson 34
Strengthening Math Skills, SV 9781419039027

LESSON **35** Multiplying Decimals by 1, 10, and 100

You can use patterns to help you multiply decimals.

If you multiply a decimal by 1, the decimal does not change.

$$2.35 \times 1 = 2.35$$

To multiply a decimal by 10 or 100, move the decimal point in the answer to the right as many places as there are zeros in the multiplier.

$$2.35 \times 10 = 23.5 \quad \text{1 zero in multiplier}$$

$$2.35 \times 100 = 235.0 \quad \text{2 zeros in multiplier}$$

Sometimes you may need to write zeros at the end of the answer to move the decimal point the correct number of places.

$$23.5 \times 100 = 2,350.0$$

Multiply. 11.17 × 100 = __________

STEP 1 Count the number of zeros in the multiplier.

There are 2 zeros in the multiplier, 100.

STEP 2 Move the decimal point in the decimal 2 places to the right.

$$11.17$$

So, 11.17 × 100 = 1,117.0

ON YOUR OWN

Multiply.

$$7.89 \times 10 = \underline{\qquad}$$

Fractions, Decimals, and Perc...
Strengthening M...

Practice

Building Skills

Complete each pattern.

To multiply a decimal by 10 or 100, move the decimal point to the right as many places as there are zeros in the multiplier.

1. $1 \times 13.65 = 13.65$

$10 \times 13.65 =$ __________

$100 \times 13.65 =$ __________

2. $1 \times 83.2 = 83.2$

$10 \times 83.2 =$ __________

$100 \times 83.2 =$ __________

Find each product.

3. $10 \times 1.01 =$ __________

4. $28.2 \times 1 =$ __________

5. $100 \times 39.37 =$ __________

6. $10 \times 6.75 =$ __________

7. $20.01 \times 100 =$ __________

8. $10 \times 0.04 =$ __________

9. $10 \times 4.54 =$ __________

10. $100 \times 13.31 =$ __________

Problem Solving

Solve.

11. Dara has some paper clips. Each paper clip is 1.25 inches long. If she makes a chain of 100 paper clips, how long will her chain be?

12. Samuel is making masks. He will put 0.65 ounce of glitter on each mask. If he makes 10 masks, how much glitter will he need?

LESSON **36** Multiplying Decimals by Decimals

Multiply a decimal by a decimal in the same way you multiply a decimal by a whole number. You do not need to line up the decimal points. Just find the product. Then count the number of decimal places in both factors. Write the decimal point in the product that many places from the right.

Example

Multiply. $4.5 \times 3.3 =$ _______________

STEP 1 Multiply. Ignore the decimal point for now.

$$\begin{array}{r} 4.5 \\ \times\ 3.3 \\ \hline 1485 \end{array}$$

STEP 2 Count the number of decimal places in both factors.

$$\begin{array}{r} 4.5 \\ \times\ 3.3 \\ \hline 1485 \end{array}$$

4.5 ← There is 1 decimal place in this factor.
× 3.3 ← There is 1 decimal place in this factor.

There is a total of 2 decimal places in the 2 factors.

STEP 3 Start at the right side of the product. Count 2 places to the left and write the decimal point there.

$$\begin{array}{r} 4.5 \\ \times\ 3.3 \\ \hline 14.85 \end{array}$$

14.85 ← Put 2 decimal places in the product.

So, $4.5 \times 3.3 = 14.85$

ON YOUR OWN

Multiply. Show your work.

$$1.2 \times 2.1 = \text{\_\_\_\_\_\_\_\_\_\_\_}$$

Practice

Building Skills

Write the decimal point in each product.

1. $3.9 \times 0.25 = 0\ 9\ 7\ 5$

2. $1.61 \times 2.7 = 4\ 3\ 4\ 7$

3. $0.5 \times 9.8 = 4\ 9\ 0$

4. $4.53 \times 2.7 = 1\ 2\ 2\ 3\ 1$

Find the product.

5.
$$\begin{array}{r} 1.1 \\ \times\ 2.3 \\ \hline \end{array}$$

6.
$$\begin{array}{r} 4.5\ 6 \\ \times\ 5.1 \\ \hline \end{array}$$

7.
$$\begin{array}{r} 0.7 \\ \times\ 0.9 \\ \hline \end{array}$$

8.
$$\begin{array}{r} 0.7\ 5 \\ \times\ 5.8 \\ \hline \end{array}$$

9.
$$\begin{array}{r} 8.9\ 9 \\ \times\ 2.5 \\ \hline \end{array}$$

10.
$$\begin{array}{r} 3.6\ 4 \\ \times\ 0.8 \\ \hline \end{array}$$

Problem Solving

Solve.

11. Gena is making a poster for her science project. The poster is 2.5 feet long by 2.25 feet wide. What is the area of the poster in square feet?
(Area = length × width)

12. A car gets 31.7 miles per gallon. Its gas tank holds 14.5 gallons. How far can the car go on a full tank of gas?

LESSON 37 Zeros in the Product

Remember, the number of decimal places in the product equals the sum of the decimal places in the factors. When you multiply two decimals, sometimes you must add zeros to the product to have the correct number of decimal places.

Write one zero between the decimal point and the 8 to show two decimal places.

$$
\begin{array}{rcl}
1 \text{ decimal place} & \rightarrow & 0.2 \\
+\ 1 \text{ decimal place} & \rightarrow & \times\ 0.4 \\
\hline
2 \text{ decimal places} & \rightarrow & 0.08
\end{array}
$$

You may have to add more than one zero in a product.

Example

Multiply. $0.36 \times 0.05 =$ _____________

STEP 1 Multiply. Ignore the decimal point for now.

$$
\begin{array}{r}
0.36 \\
\times\ 0.05 \\
\hline
180
\end{array}
$$

STEP 2 Count the number of decimal places in both factors.

0.36 ← There are 2 decimal places in this factor.
$\times\ 0.05$ ← There are 2 decimal places in this factor.
180

There is a total of 4 decimal places in the two factors. You need 4 decimal places in the product.

STEP 3 You have only 3 decimal places in the product, so you must add a zero in the tenths place. You should also put a zero in the ones place.

$$
\begin{array}{r}
0.36 \\
\times\ 0.05 \\
\hline
0.0180
\end{array}
$$

So, $0.36 \times 0.05 = 0.0180$

ON YOUR OWN

Multiply. Show your work.

$$0.52 \times 0.11 = \text{\_\_\_\_\_\_\_\_\_\_\_\_}$$

Practice

Building Skills

Write the decimal point in each product.

> If you have more decimal places in your factors than in your product, you must add one or more zeros to your product.

1. $1.3 \times 0.02 = 0\,0\,2\,6$ **2.** $2.40 \times 0.01 = 0\,0\,2\,4$

3. $25.4 \times 0.04 = 1\,0\,1\,6$ **4.** $0.2 \times 0.3 = 0\,0\,6$

Find the product. Add a zero to the product if necessary.

5. $\begin{array}{r} 0.3\,3 \\ \times\ 0.1 \\ \hline \end{array}$ **6.** $\begin{array}{r} 0.2 \\ \times 0.2\,1 \\ \hline \end{array}$ **7.** $\begin{array}{r} 0.1\,1 \\ \times\ 0.1 \\ \hline \end{array}$

8. $\begin{array}{r} 0.2\,5 \\ \times\ 0.4 \\ \hline \end{array}$ **9.** $\begin{array}{r} 0.4\,6 \\ \times 0.1\,4 \\ \hline \end{array}$ **10.** $\begin{array}{r} 0.6 \\ \times 0.1\,3 \\ \hline \end{array}$

Problem Solving

Solve.

11. The backward walk race was 0.1 kilometer long. Bob had already finished 0.25 of the race. What part of a kilometer had Bob gone?

12. A bowl contained 0.3 quart of soup. Karla ate 0.3 of the soup. How much of a quart did Karla eat?

LESSON 38

Dividing Decimals by Whole Numbers

Divide a decimal by a whole number in the same way you divide whole numbers. Before you begin to divide, place the decimal point in the quotient above the decimal point in the dividend. Then divide as you would with whole numbers.

Example

Divide. 2.65 ÷ 5 = _______

STEP 1 Set up the problem using a division bracket.

$$5\overline{)2.65}$$

STEP 2 Place a decimal point in the quotient directly above the decimal point in the dividend.

$$5\overline{)2.65}$$

STEP 3 Divide as with whole numbers.

$$\begin{array}{r} 0.53 \\ 5\overline{)2.65} \\ -2\,5 \\ \hline 15 \\ -15 \\ \hline 0 \end{array}$$

Add a zero to the left of the decimal point as a placeholder.

So, 2.65 ÷ 5 = 0.53

ON YOUR OWN

Divide. Show your work.

3.24 ÷ 4 = _______

Name _________________________________ Date _____________________

Practice

> To divide a fraction by a whole number, write a decimal point in the quotient directly above the decimal point in the dividend. Then divide as you would with whole numbers.

Building Skills

Write the decimal point in each quotient.

1. $$2\overline{)1.56}$$ quotient 078

2. $$6\overline{)12.48}$$ quotient 208

3. $$5\overline{)15.25}$$ quotient 305

Find the quotient. Remember to write the decimal point in each quotient.

4. $$3\overline{)4.8}$$

5. $$8\overline{)7.2}$$

6. $$2\overline{)2.2}$$

7. $$5\overline{)4.95}$$

8. $$7\overline{)21.42}$$

9. $$9\overline{)36.81}$$

Problem Solving

Solve.

10. Keri uses 12.75 cups of flour to make cookies for the bake sale. If she makes 3 batches of cookies, how much flour does she use for each batch?

11. A box of tacos weighs 40.5 ounces. If there are 9 tacos in the box, how many ounces does each taco weigh?

12. The art teacher has 7.5 yards of fabric. If she divides the fabric equally among 6 students, how many yards of fabric will each student get?

LESSON 39 — Dividing Decimals by 1, 10, and 100

You can use patterns to help you divide decimals.

If you divide a decimal by 1, the decimal does not change.

$$1.25 \div 1 = 1.25$$

To divide a decimal by 10 or 100, move the decimal point in the answer to the left as many places as there are zeros in the divisor.

$$1.25 \div 10 = 0.125 \quad \text{one zero in divisor}$$

Sometimes you may need to write zeros in the tenths place to move the decimal point the correct number of places.

$$1.25 \div 100 = 0.0125 \quad \text{two zeros in divisor}$$

Divide. $10.25 \div 100 =$ _________

STEP 1 Count the number of zeros in the divisor.

There are 2 zeros in the divisor, 100.

STEP 2 Move the decimal point in the decimal 2 places to the left.

$$10.25$$

You should add a zero in the ones place as a placeholder.

So, $10.25 \div 100 = 0.1025$

(ON YOUR OWN)

Divide.

$$8.75 \div 10 = \text{_________}$$

Practice

Building Skills

Complete each pattern.

> To divide a decimal by 10 or 100, move the decimal point to the left as many places as there are zeros in the divisor.

1. $7.5 \div 1 = 7.5$

$7.5 \div 10 =$ _________

$7.5 \div 100 =$ _________

2. $3.33 \div 1 = 3.33$

$3.33 \div 10 =$ _________

$3.33 \div 100 =$ _________

Find each quotient.

3. $1.1 \div 1 =$ _________

4. $23.2 \div 10 =$ _________

5. $37.93 \div 100 =$ _________

6. $0.76 \div 10 =$ _________

7. $3.45 \div 10 =$ _________

8. $17.43 \div 100 =$ _________

9. $3.87 \div 100 =$ _________

10. $0.05 \div 10 =$ _________

Problem Solving

Solve.

11. A bag of beads weighs 35.5 grams. There are 100 beads in the bag. How many grams does each bead weigh?

12. Heather has 195.5 inches of necklace chain. She wants to make 10 necklaces. How long can each necklace be?

Fractions, Decimals, and Percents: Unit 2: Lesson 39
Strengthening Math Skills, SV 9781419039027

LESSON ④ Adding and Subtracting Money

You know about money. Did you know that money uses decimals?

One dollar = 100 pennies = $1.00

One dime = 10 pennies = 0.1 = $0.10

1 penny = 0.01 = $0.01

You can add and subtract money just as you add and subtract decimals. When you add and subtract money, you must line up the decimal points. Then you add or subtract as you would regular decimals or whole numbers.

Example

Add. $8.25 + $3.90 = __________

STEP 1 Set up your problem vertically. Line up the decimal points.

$$\begin{array}{r} \$8.25 \\ + \ \$3.90 \\ \hline \end{array}$$

STEP 2 Put a decimal point in the answer directly under the other decimal points.

$$\begin{array}{r} \$8.25 \\ + \ \$3.90 \\ \hline . \end{array}$$

STEP 3 Add. Regroup if necessary.

$$\begin{array}{r} \overset{1}{}\$8.25 \\ + \ \$3.90 \\ \hline \$12.15 \end{array}$$

When you add the tenths place, you must regroup. Move 1 to the ones place.

So, $8.25 + $3.90 = $12.15

(ON YOUR OWN)

Add. Show your work.

$1.43 + $2.95 = __________

Practice

> To add or subtract money, first line up the decimal points. Then add or subtract as you would regular decimals or whole numbers.

Building Skills

Find the sum or difference.

1. $3.25
+ $2.25

2. $0.17
+ $7.98

3. $11.55
+ $12.45

4. $7.65
− $3.23

5. $19.94
− $5.57

6. $1.19
− $0.39

7. $43.77
+ $1.49

8. $4.33
− $3.34

9. $10.15
+ $15.86

Problem Solving

Add or subtract to solve.

10. Marta bought two CDs. One cost $14.78 and the other cost $16.49. How much did Marta spend on the two CDs?

11. Allison had $78.90 in her savings account. She withdrew $25.25 to buy a gift for her grandmother. How much money did Allison have left in her savings account?

12. Terrell is saving money for his summer vacation. He saved $15.65 in February, $22.75 in March, and $19.15 in April. How much has he saved so far?

Multiplying and Dividing Money by Whole Numbers

LESSON 41

Multiply money by whole numbers in the same way you multiply decimals by whole numbers. Find the product and then count the number of decimal places in the money factor. Place the decimal point in the product that many places from the right. Be sure to add a dollar sign to the answer.

$$\$1.50 \times 5 = \$7.50$$

Divide money by whole numbers in the same way you divide decimals by whole numbers. Before you begin to divide, place the decimal point in the quotient above the decimal point in the money dividend. Then divide as you would with whole numbers. Be sure to add a dollar sign to the answer.

$$\$7.50 \div 5 = \$1.50$$

Example

Divide. $10.00 ÷ 4 = ___________

STEP 1 Set up the problem using a division bracket.

$$4\overline{)\$1\,0.0\,0}$$

STEP 2 Place a decimal point in the quotient directly above the decimal point in the dividend.

$$4\overline{)\$1\,0.0\,0}$$

STEP 3 Divide as with whole numbers.

$$
\begin{array}{r}
\$2.5\,0 \\
4\overline{)\$1\,0.0\,0} \\
-\ 8 \\
\hline
2\,0 \\
-\ 2\,0 \\
\hline
0\,0 \\
-\ 0 \\
\hline
0
\end{array}
$$

Add a dollar sign to the quotient.

So, $10.00 ÷ 4 = $2.50

ON YOUR OWN

Divide. Show your work.

$$\$6.50 \div 2 = ___________$$

Practice

Multiply and divide money by whole numbers the same way you multiply and divide decimals by whole numbers.

Building Skills

Find the product or quotient. Remember to add a dollar sign to the answer.

1. $3.25
      ×   3

2. $5.50
      ×   4

3. $0.75
      ×   2

4. 8)$8.80

5. 5)$13.60

6. 3)$1.05

7. $15.30
      ×   7

8. 6)$42.96

9. $6.19
      × 10

Problem Solving

Solve.

10. Justin bought 2 baseballs for $2.59 each. How much did he pay for the two baseballs altogether?

11. Justin also bought 3 pairs of socks for a total of $5.55. How much did each pair of socks cost?

12. At the ball game, Justin bought 5 drinks for his friends. Each drink cost $0.85. How much did the 5 drinks cost altogether?

LESSON 42   What Is Percent?

Percent means *per hundred*. The symbol for percent is %. When using percents, the whole is divided into 100 equal parts. A percent, then, is some part of one hundred. However, some percents can be larger than 100% or smaller than 1%.

A percent is a ratio in which the denominator is 100. 35% means 35 hundredths, 0.35, or $\frac{35}{100}$.

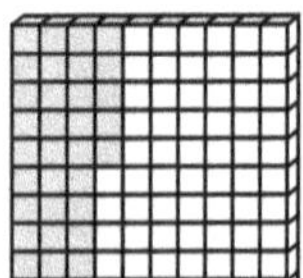

Ratio $= \frac{35}{100}$
Decimal $= 0.35$
Percent $= 35\%$

Example

What percent of the blocks are shaded?

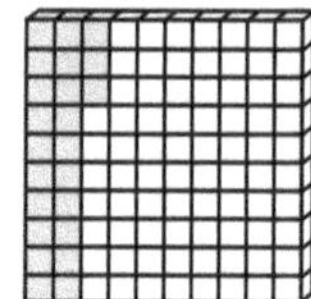

STEP 1 Count the number of blocks in the square.

There are 100 blocks in the square.

STEP 2 Count the number of blocks that are shaded.

23 of the blocks are shaded.

STEP 3 Write the number of shaded blocks as a ratio.

23 of 100 blocks are shaded, so the ratio is $\frac{23}{100}$.

STEP 4 Write the ratio as a percent. $\frac{23}{100} = 23\%$

So, 23% of the blocks are shaded.

ON YOUR OWN

What percent of the blocks are shaded? Write your answer as a ratio and a percent.

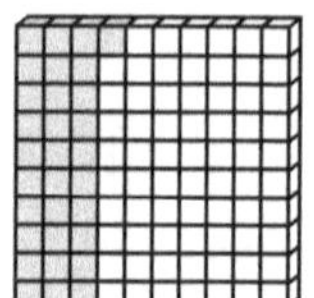

Fractions, Decimals, and Percents: Unit 3: Lesson 42
Strengthening Math Skills, SV 9781419039027

Practice

Building Skills

A percent is a ratio. The symbol for percent is %.

Complete.

1. Ratio = $\frac{17}{100}$

Decimal = 0.17

Percent = __________

2. Ratio = $\frac{89}{100}$

Decimal = __________

Percent = __________

3. Ratio = __________

Decimal = 0.63

Percent = __________

Write the percent that tells what part is shaded. Remember to include the % symbol.

4. 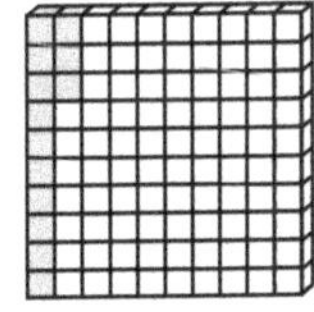

____

5. 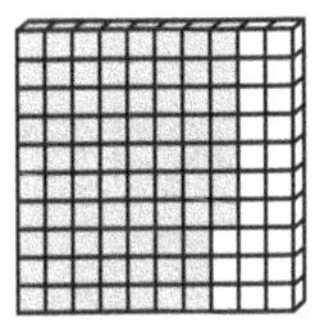

____

6. 

____

Problem Solving

Solve.

7. Merry's kitchen floor has 100 tiles. 41 of the tiles are black, and the rest of the tiles are white. What percent of all the floor tiles are black? Write your answer as a ratio and a percent.

8. Brad took a math test. There were 100 problems on the test. Brad got 83 of the problems correct. What percent of all the problems did Brad get correct?

LESSON 43 — Using Mental Math to Find Percent

The following chart shows some ways to use mental math to find certain percents.

Percent	Fraction	Think	Example
200%	$\frac{2}{1}$	Multiply by 2.	200% of 10 = 2 × 10 = 20
100%	$\frac{1}{1}$	Multiply by 1.	100% of 3 = 1 × 3 = 3
50%	$\frac{1}{2}$	Multiply by $\frac{1}{2}$ or divide by 2.	50% of 8 = 8 ÷ 2 = 4
25%	$\frac{1}{4}$	Multiply by $\frac{1}{4}$ or divide by 4.	25% of 16 = 16 ÷ 4 = 4
10%	$\frac{1}{10}$	Multiply by $\frac{1}{10}$ or divide by 10 or move the decimal point one place to the left.	10% of 460 = 46.0 = 46

Example

Use mental math to find 25% of 12.

STEP 1 Review the chart.

The chart says to find 25% of a number, multiply by $\frac{1}{4}$ or divide by 4.

STEP 2 Multiply $12 \times \frac{1}{4}$.

$$\frac{12}{1} \times \frac{1}{4} = \frac{12}{4} = 3$$

STEP 3 To check your answer, divide 12 by 4.

$$12 \div 4 = 3$$

So, 25% of 12 is 3.

ON YOUR OWN

Use mental math to find 50% of 14.

Practice

> Use mental math when possible to help you work with percents.

Building Skills

Complete each sentence.

1. To find 25% of a number, you would ____________ by 4.

2. To find ____________ of a number, you would multiply by $\frac{1}{2}$.

3. To find 20% of a number, you would multiply by ____________.

Use mental math to solve each problem.

4. 200% of 100 = ______

    ______ × 100 = ______

5. 50% of 10 = ______

    10 ÷ ______ = ______

6. 10% of 30 = ______

    30 × ______ = ______

7. 25% of 20 = ______

8. 10% of 10 = ______

9. 20% of 10 = ______

10. 25% of 100 = ______

11. 50% of 50 = ______

12. 200% of 15 = ______

Problem Solving

Use mental math to solve.

13. Cory had 40 stamps. He put 50% of them in his stamp book. How many stamps did Cory put in his stamp book?

14. Shawna has 50 CDs. Of these, 10% are by her favorite group, The Goobers. How many of Shawna's CDs are by The Goobers?

15. Mr. Cox collects clocks. He has 32 clocks in his collection. Of these, 25% do not work. How many of Mr. Cox's clocks don't work?

Name _______________________________________ Date _______________________

LESSON **44** Changing Decimals to Percents

Changing a decimal to a percent is very easy. To change a decimal to a percent, move the decimal point 2 places to the right. Or you can multiply the decimal by 100. Then write the percent symbol (%). Add or drop zeros if necessary.

$$0.50 \longrightarrow 50\%$$
$$0.05 \longrightarrow 5\%$$

Example

In Sindi's class, 0.65 of the students do not want to go to school through July. What percent of the students do not want to go to school through July?

STEP 1 Multiply the decimal by 100. Multiplying by 100 moves the decimal point 2 places to the right.

$$0.65 \times 100 = 65.0$$

STEP 2 Add the percent symbol.

$$65\%$$

So, 0.65 = 65%

ON YOUR OWN

A survey found that 0.83 of the students at Scully School want to have a Fall Fair. What percent of the students want to have a Fall Fair?
Show your work.

Practice

> To change a decimal to a percent, just move the decimal point 2 places to the right.

Building Skills

Write each decimal as a percent. Remember to add the percent symbol.

1. 0.75 = _________

2. 0.12 = _________

3. 0.41 = _________

4. 0.6 = _________

5. 0.9 = _________

6. 0.3 = _________

7. 0.02 = _________

8. 0.08 = _________

9. 0.04 = _________

10. 1.15 = _________

11. 2.27 = _________

12. 3.50 = _________

Problem Solving

Solve.

13. On a history test, Jessica got 0.87 of the answers correct. What percent of the answers did Jessica get correct?

14. Jarett learned that 0.33 of the students in his class want to become teachers. What percent of the students want to become teachers?

15. Teesha took a survey of the students in her class. 0.3 of the students thought they should have more homework. What percent of the students <u>did not</u> think they should have more homework?

LESSON **45** Changing Percents to Decimals

Sometimes, problems are easier to solve if you change percents to decimals. You can write any percent as a decimal.

- First remove the percent symbol. Add a decimal point if needed. A decimal point added to the right of a whole number does not change its value.

- Move the decimal point 2 places to the left. Sometimes you will need to add a zero as a placeholder.

$$35\% = 0.35 \qquad 7\% = 0.07$$

Example

In one class, 3% of the students said they liked spinach sandwiches better than cake. What is 3% written as a decimal?

STEP 1 Remove the percent symbol and add a decimal to the right of the number.

$$3\% = 3$$

STEP 2 Move the decimal point 2 places to the left. You must add a zero before the 3.

$$3. \longrightarrow 0.03$$

You should also write a 0 to the left of the decimal point in the ones place.

So, 3% written as a decimal is 0.03.

ON YOUR OWN

In Jesse's class, 20% of the students missed a question on the reading test. What is 20% written as a decimal? Show your work.

Fractions, Decimals, and Percents: Unit 3: Lesson 45
Strengthening Math Skills, SV 9781419039027

Practice

> To change a percent to a decimal, remove the percent symbol and move the decimal point 2 places to the left.

Building Skills

Write each percent as a decimal. Remember to remove the percent symbol and add the decimal point.

1. 84% = __________

2. 19% = __________

3. 43% = __________

4. 5% = __________

5. 1% = __________

6. 9% = __________

7. 14% = __________

8. 40% = __________

9. 3.5% = __________

10. 125% = __________

11. 100% = __________

12. 250% = __________

Problem Solving

Solve.

13. A group of friends read the same book, and 50% of them said they liked the book. What is 50% written as a decimal?

14. The book was made into a movie, and 80% of the friends said they liked the book better than the movie. What is 80% written as a decimal?

15. The price of movie tickets went up 150% over 5 years. What is 150% written as a decimal?

LESSON **46** Changing Fractions to Percents

Fractions can be easily changed to percents. Remember, a percent is a ratio in which the denominator is 100. A ratio is often written as a fraction.

To change a fraction to a percent, first change the fraction to a decimal. To do this, divide the numerator by the denominator. Then rewrite the decimal quotient as a percent by moving the decimal point 2 places to the right. Add a zero if necessary.

$$\frac{4}{5} = 0.80 = 80\% \qquad \frac{1}{10} = 0.1 = 10\%$$

Example

Allison took a test. She got 6 out of 8 questions correct. What percent of the questions did Allison get correct?

STEP 1 Set up the ratio as a fraction.

Allison got 6 out of 8 questions correct $= \frac{6}{8}$

STEP 2 Divide the numerator by the denominator.

$$6 \div 8 = 0.75$$

STEP 3 Move the decimal point 2 places to the right. Then write the percent symbol.

$$0.75 = 75\%$$

So, Allison got 75% of the questions correct.

ON YOUR OWN

**Chet played a game. He hit 9 out of 10 targets.
What percent of the targets did Chet hit?
Show your work.**

Practice

Building Skills

Write each fraction as a percent. Add zeros if needed.
Remember to add the percent symbol.

> To change a fraction to a percent, divide the numerator by the denominator. Then move the decimal point 2 places to the right and add the percent symbol.

1. $\frac{5}{10} =$ _____________

2. $\frac{77}{100} =$ _____________

3. $\frac{33}{100} =$ _____________

4. $\frac{10}{5} =$ _____________

5. $\frac{3}{5} =$ _____________

6. $\frac{15}{20} =$ _____________

7. $\frac{1}{4} =$ _____________

8. $\frac{1}{5} =$ _____________

9. $\frac{3}{4} =$ _____________

Problem Solving

Solve.

10. Six of the 10 students in the cafeteria line got pizza for lunch. What percent of the students in line got pizza?

11. Two out of 5 people at the zoo visited the snake pit. What percent of the people at the zoo visited the snake pit?

12. At recess, 25 of the 50 students played basketball. What percent of the students at recess played basketball?

LESSON 47 Changing Percents to Fractions

Changing a percent to a fraction is easier than changing a fraction to a percent. Remember, *percent* means "per hundred." So any percent can be written in the fraction form $\frac{n}{100}$.

To write a percent as a fraction:

- remove the percent symbol.
- write the percent as a fraction with a denominator of 100.
- simplify the fraction if possible.

Example

Thirty percent of the students in Britney's class bring their lunch to school. What fraction of the students bring their lunch to school?

STEP 1 Remove the percent symbol. Then write the percent as a fraction with a denominator of 100.

$$30\% = \frac{30}{100}$$

STEP 2 Simplify the fraction if possible.

Divide the numerator and denominator by their greatest common factor (GCF).

Factors of 30 are 1, 2, 3, 5, 6, **10**, 15, 30.

Factors of 100 are 1, 2, 4, 5, **10**, 20, 25, 50, 100.

The GCF of 30 and 100 is 10.

$$\frac{30}{100} \longrightarrow \frac{30 \div 10}{100 \div 10} \longrightarrow \frac{3}{10}$$

So, $\frac{3}{10}$ of the students bring their lunch to school.

ON YOUR OWN

Sixty percent of the students at Britney's school took part in the food drive. What fraction of the students took part in the food drive? Show your work.

Practice

Building Skills

Write each percent as a fraction. Simplify if possible.

> To change a percent to a fraction, write the percent as a fraction with a denominator of 100. Then simplify the fraction if possible.

1. 10% = _____________

2. 50% = _____________

3. 25% = _____________

4. 100% = _____________

5. 66% = _____________

6. 8% = _____________

7. 75% = _____________

8. 48% = _____________

9. 55% = _____________

10. 1% = _____________

11. 120% = _____________

12. 250% = _____________

Problem Solving

Solve.

13. Mora works at the grocery store. She saves 35% of her pay for school clothes. What fraction of her pay does she save?

14. Alberto finished 40% of his math problems before recess. What fraction of the problems did he finish before recess?

15. Mr. Farmer planted 85% of his seeds before he took a break. What fraction of his seeds did he plant before he took a break?

LESSON ㊽ Finding the Part

What if you need to know what 30% of 60 is? You are looking for a part. How would you find the answer? You can use the percent triangle to help you find the missing part.

Look at the triangle. To find the part, cover the word *part*. The remaining pieces are connected by a multiplication sign. Multiply the pieces you have to find the part.

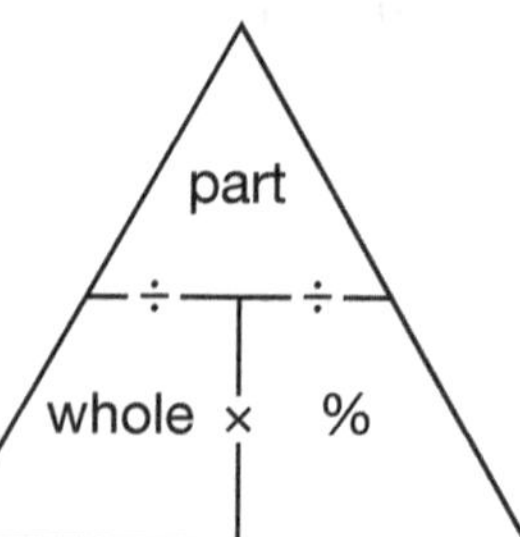

Example

What is 30% of 60?

STEP 1 Identify the pieces you have.

30% is the percent. 60 is the whole.

STEP 2 Write a percent sentence.

$$\text{part} = \text{whole} \times \text{percent}$$

STEP 3 Replace the words with numbers.

$$\text{part} = 60 \times 30\%$$

STEP 4 Multiply. Remember to change your percent to a decimal.

$$60 \times 30\% = 60 \times 0.30 = 18.00 = 18$$

So, 30% of 60 is 18.

ON YOUR OWN

Use the percent triangle to find 40% of 50. Show your work.

Fractions, Decimals, and Percents: Unit 3: Lesson 48
Strengthening Math Skills, SV 9781419039027

Practice

> Use the percent triangle to help you find a percent of a number.

Building Skills

Find the percent of each number.

1. 25% of 32 = __________

2. 5% of 40 = __________

3. 60% of 50 = __________

4. 10% of 90 = __________

5. 50% of 100 = __________

6. 35% of 200 = __________

7. 90% of 90 = __________

8. 15% of 400 = __________

9. 150% of 48 = __________

10. 100% of 1 = __________

Problem Solving

Solve.

11. Carl's Car Lot had 70 cars. A hailstorm damaged 60% of the cars. How many cars were damaged by the hailstorm?

12. In a baseball game, Pablo threw 88 pitches. Of these pitches, 75% were strikes. How many strikes did Pablo throw?

Fractions, Decimals, and Percents: Unit 3: Lesson 48
Strengthening Math Skills, SV 9781419039027

LESSON ⑨ Finding the Whole

When you solve percent problems, you are looking for a missing piece. The percent triangle helps you to find that missing piece. A percent triangle shows how the three pieces are related.

Sometimes you will be asked to find the whole. The percent triangle can help you. To find the whole, cover the word *whole*. The remaining parts are connected with a division sign. Divide the part by the percent to find the whole. Remember to rewrite the percent as a decimal before you divide.

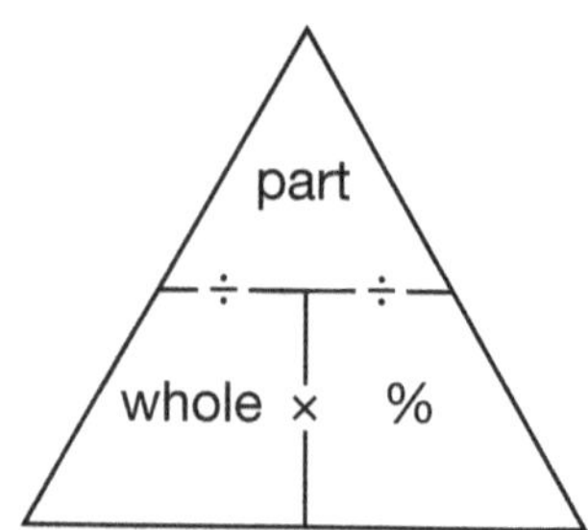

Example

40 is 50% of what number?

STEP 1 Identify the pieces you have.

40 is the part. 50% is the percent.

STEP 2 Write a percent sentence.

whole = part ÷ percent

STEP 3 Replace the words with numbers.

whole = 40 ÷ 50%

STEP 4 Divide to find the answer. Remember to change the percent to a decimal.

40 ÷ 50% = 40 ÷ 0.50 = 80

So, 40 is 50% of 80.

ON YOUR OWN

20 is 40% of what number? Show your work.

Practice

Building Skills

Find the whole. Show your work.

1. 6 is 10% of what number?

2. 10 is 20% of what number?

3. 15 is 25% of what number?

4. 25 is 50% of what number?

5. 75 is 75% of what number?

6. 30 is 40% of what number?

Problem Solving

Solve.

7. 40% of the students who entered the writing contest won prizes. Eight students won prizes. How many students entered the writing contest?

8. Eighteen people were hired to work at a summer camp. This was 60% of the people who applied for jobs. How many people applied for jobs at the summer camp?

9. Mr. Corn sold 80% of his farm. The number of acres sold was 112. How many acres were in the farm before the sale?

10. The population of Goonville is now 1,428 people. This is 119% of the population last year. What was the population of Goonville last year?

LESSON 50 Finding the Percent

You have used the percent triangle to help you find the part and the whole. You can also use the triangle to help you find the percent.

To find the percent, cover the symbol for percent. The remaining pieces of the triangle are connected with a division sign. Divide the part by the whole to find the percent. The answer is a decimal. Multiply the decimal by 100 to find the percent.

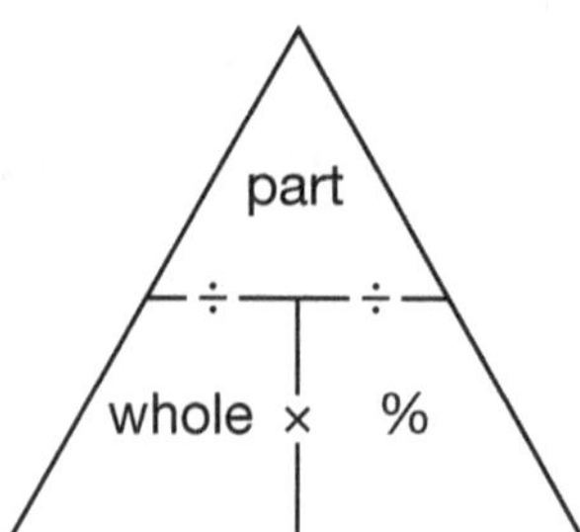

Example

30 is what percent of 150?

STEP 1 Identify the pieces you have.

30 is the part. 150 is the whole.

STEP 2 Write a percent sentence.

percent = (part ÷ whole) × 100

STEP 3 Replace the words with numbers.

percent = (30 ÷ 150) × 100

STEP 4 Divide. Then multiply by 100 and add the % symbol.

(30 ÷ 150) × 100 = 0.2 × 100 = 20%

So, 30 is 20% of 150.

ON YOUR OWN

20 is what percent of 80? Show your work.

Practice

Building Skills

Find the percent. Show your work.

1. 40 is what percent of 100?

2. What percent of 90 is 90?

3. 15 is what percent of 20?

4. 1 is what percent of 50?

5. 48 is what percent of 80?

6. What percent of 200 is 50?

Problem Solving

Solve.

7. On a math test, Jason got 72 out of 90 problems correct. What percent of the problems did Jason answer correctly?

8. One day, 36 students at Getsmart Academy were out sick. If there are 450 students at Getsmart, what percent of the students were out sick that day?

9. In a survey of 800 people, 240 people said they liked country music best. What percent of the people surveyed liked country music best?

10. On a long plane flight, 56 of 224 passengers took a nap. What percent of the passengers took a nap during the flight?

Fractions, Decimals, and Percents: Unit 3: Lesson 50
Strengthening Math Skills, SV 9781419039027

LESSON 51 Writing a Percent Equation

You have used the percent triangle to help you find missing parts in a problem. There is another way to solve percent problems. Use a **percent equation** to solve any type of percent problem. Write the equation as simply as you can. Use the **variable**, n, to stand for the missing number.

Example

A whale-watching tour spotted 30 whales. This is 60% of the total they expected to see. How many whales did they expect to see?

STEP 1 Restate the problem as simply as possible.

30 is 0.6 of what number?

STEP 2 Write the equation the way you read the problem. Use n for the missing number.

30 is 0.6 of what number?

$$30 = 0.6 \times n$$

STEP 3 Solve for n.

$$30 = 0.6 \times n$$

$$\frac{30}{0.6} = \frac{0.6}{0.6} \times n$$

$$50 = 1 \times n$$

$$50 = n$$

So, the tour expected to see 50 whales.

ON YOUR OWN

Ms. Yellar has 30 students in her class. There are 120 students in the grade. What percent of the students in the grade are in Ms. Yellar's class? Write a percent equation to solve.

Fractions, Decimals, and Percents: Unit 3: Lesson 51
Strengthening Math Skills, SV 9781419039027

Practice

Building Skills

> Write a percent equation to help you solve any kind of percent problem.

Write a percent equation for each problem. Use n for the missing number.

1. What is 10% of 50?

2. What percent of 60 is 24?

3. What is 30% of 80?

4. 80% of what number is 16?

Write a percent equation for each problem. Use n for the missing number. Then solve.

5. What is 25% of 16?

6. What percent of 12 is 9?

7. What is 80% of 80?

8. 10% of what number is 15?

Problem Solving

Write a percent equation to solve. Show your work.

9. Ryan's football team won 6 games and lost 4 games. What percent of their games did the team lose?

10. Krystal lost 12 of the coins in her collection. This was 15% of her collection. How many coins were in her collection before the loss?

LESSON 52 Finding the Final Amount

Sometimes, solving a problem takes several steps. You may have to add or subtract to find the final answer.

To find the final amount:
- Find the amount of **increase** or **decrease** by using a percent.
- Add or subtract the result to find the final amount.

For sales tax problems, add the amount of increase to the original amount. For discounts, subtract the amount of decrease from the original amount.

Example

Bert bought a bat at a discount of 20%. The original price of the bat was $15.00. For how much did Bert buy the bat? Find the final amount.

STEP 1 Find the amount of decrease (amount of discount).

$$\$15.00 \times 0.20 = \$3.00$$

STEP 2 Subtract the amount of decrease (discount) from the original price.

$$\$15.00 - \$3.00 = \$12.00$$

So, Bert bought the bat at a discounted price of $12.00. But he had to pay sales tax at a rate of 6%. What was the total amount Bert had to pay for the bat? Find the final amount.

STEP 3 Find the amount of increase (amount of tax).

$$\$12.00 \times 0.06 = \$0.72$$

STEP 4 Add the amount of increase to the original amount.

$$\$12.00 + \$0.72 = \$12.72$$

So, Bert paid the total amount of $12.72 for the bat.

ON YOUR OWN

A camera usually sells for $150. This week it is on sale. The sales price includes a discount of 30%. What is the sales price of the camera?

Fraction Circles

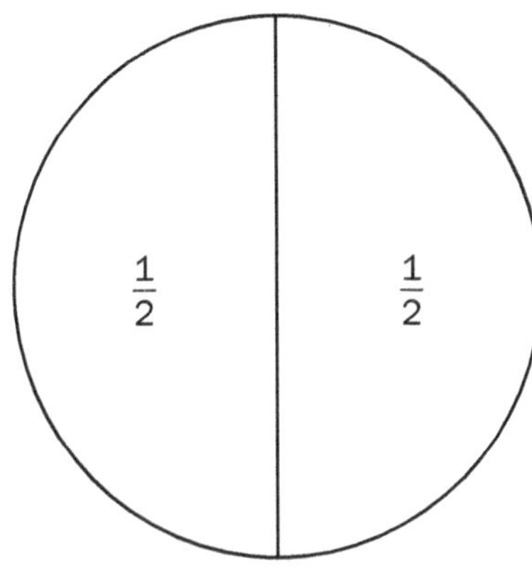
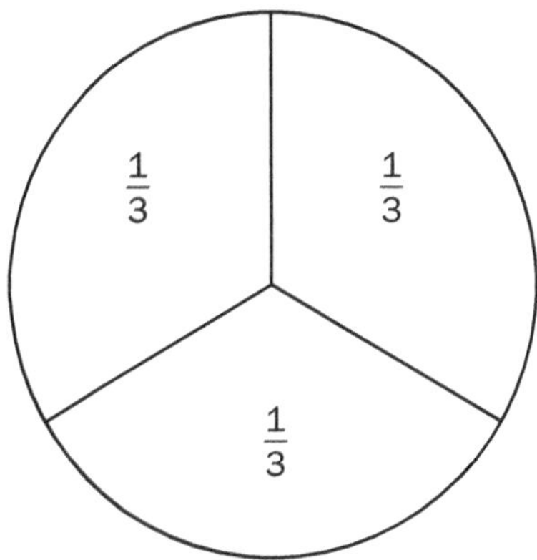
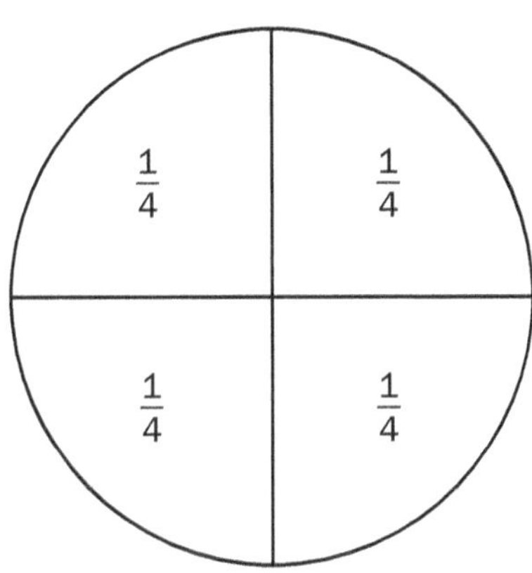
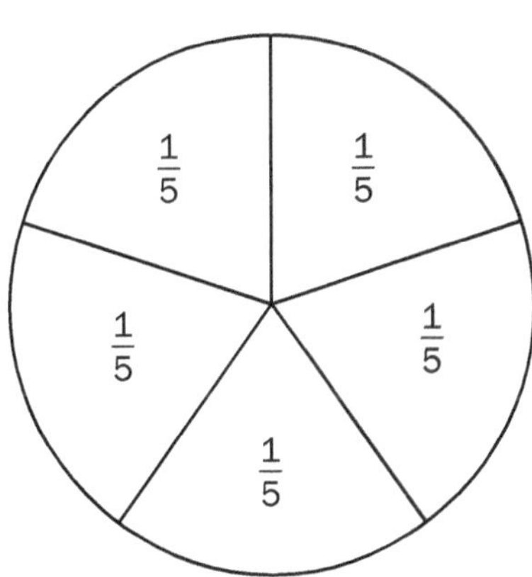
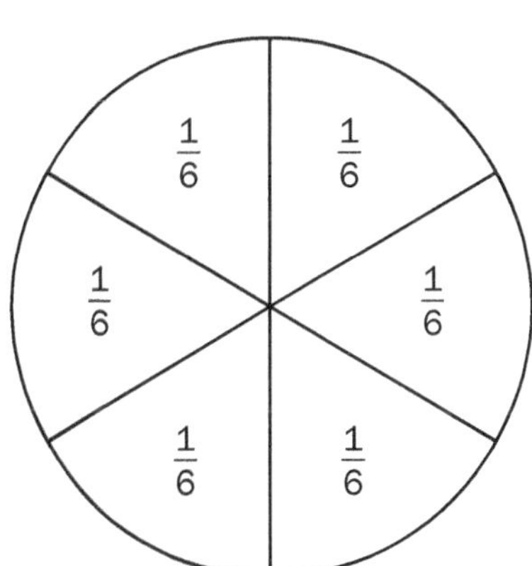
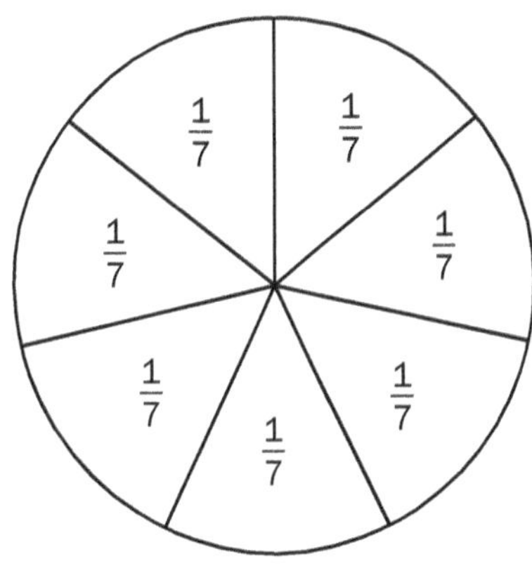
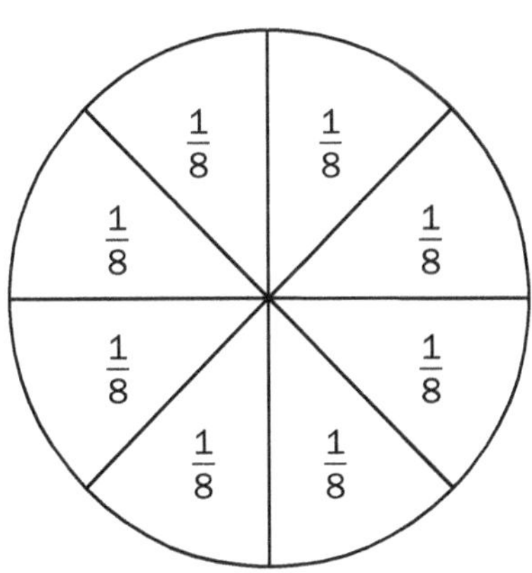
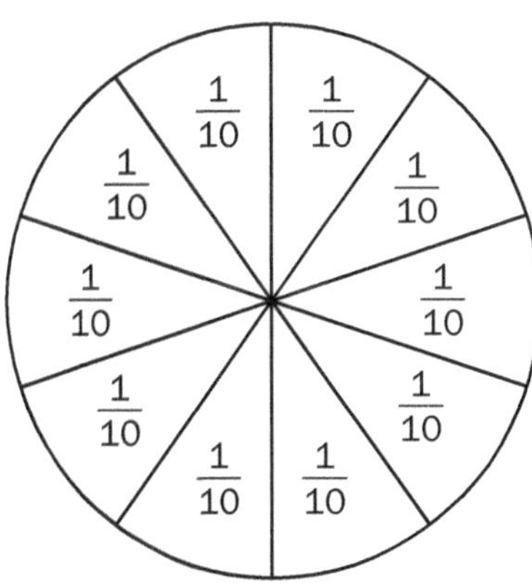

Equivalent Fractions, Decimals, and Percents

Use the chart to find equivalents among fractions, decimals, and percents.
Hint: A short line above a number means that number keeps repeating.

Fraction	Decimal	Percent
$\frac{1}{2}$	0.5	50%
$\frac{2}{2} = 1$	1.0	100%

Fraction	Decimal	Percent
$\frac{1}{8}$	0.125	12.5%
$\frac{2}{8} = \frac{1}{4}$	0.25	25%
$\frac{3}{8}$	0.375	37.5%
$\frac{4}{8} = \frac{1}{2}$	0.5	50%
$\frac{5}{8}$	0.625	62.5%
$\frac{6}{8} = \frac{3}{4}$	0.75	75%
$\frac{7}{8}$	0.875	87.5%
$\frac{8}{8} = 1$	1.0	100%

Fraction	Decimal	Percent
$\frac{1}{3}$	$0.33\overline{3}$	$33.\overline{3}\%$
$\frac{2}{3}$	$0.66\overline{6}$	$66.\overline{6}\%$
$\frac{3}{3} = 1$	1.0	100%

Fraction	Decimal	Percent
$\frac{1}{4}$	0.25	25%
$\frac{2}{4} = \frac{1}{2}$	0.5	50%
$\frac{3}{4}$	0.75	75%
$\frac{4}{4} = 1$	1.0	100%

Fraction	Decimal	Percent
$\frac{1}{10}$	0.1	10%
$\frac{2}{10} = \frac{1}{5}$	0.2	20%
$\frac{3}{10}$	0.3	30%
$\frac{4}{10} = \frac{2}{5}$	0.4	40%
$\frac{5}{10} = \frac{1}{2}$	0.5	50%
$\frac{6}{10} = \frac{3}{5}$	0.6	60%
$\frac{7}{10}$	0.7	70%
$\frac{8}{10} = \frac{4}{5}$	0.8	80%
$\frac{9}{10}$	0.9	90%
$\frac{10}{10} = 1$	1.0	100%

Fraction	Decimal	Percent
$\frac{1}{5}$	0.2	20%
$\frac{2}{5}$	0.4	40%
$\frac{3}{5}$	0.6	60%
$\frac{4}{5}$	0.8	80%
$\frac{5}{5} = 1$	1.0	100%

Fraction	Decimal	Percent
$\frac{1}{100}$	0.01	1%
1	1.0	100%

Fraction	Decimal	Percent
$\frac{1}{6}$	$0.16\overline{6}$	$16.\overline{6}\%$
$\frac{2}{6} = \frac{1}{3}$	$0.33\overline{3}$	$33.\overline{3}\%$
$\frac{3}{6} = \frac{1}{2}$	0.5	50%
$\frac{4}{6} = \frac{2}{3}$	$0.66\overline{6}$	$66.\overline{6}\%$
$\frac{5}{6}$	$0.83\overline{3}$	$83.\overline{3}\%$
$\frac{6}{6} = 1$	1.0	100%

Percents and Problem Solving

Find the Part

Given:	the percent and the whole
Equation:	Whole × Percent = Part
Example:	Find 30% of 120.
	120 × 0.30 = 36

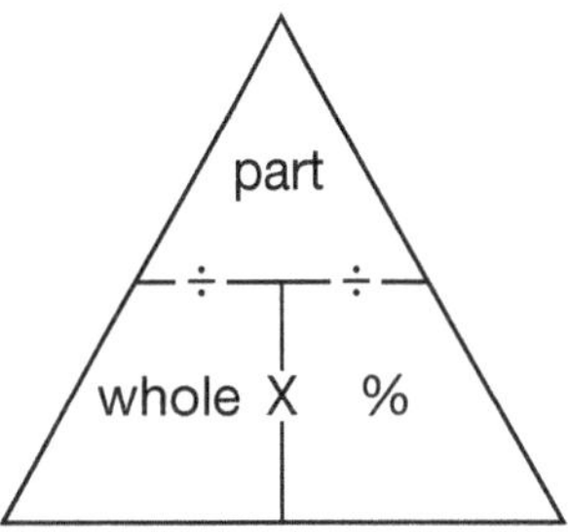

Find the Percent

Given:	the part and the whole
Equation:	(Part ÷ Whole) × 100 = Percent
Example:	50 is what percent of 250?
	(50 ÷ 250) × 100 = 20%

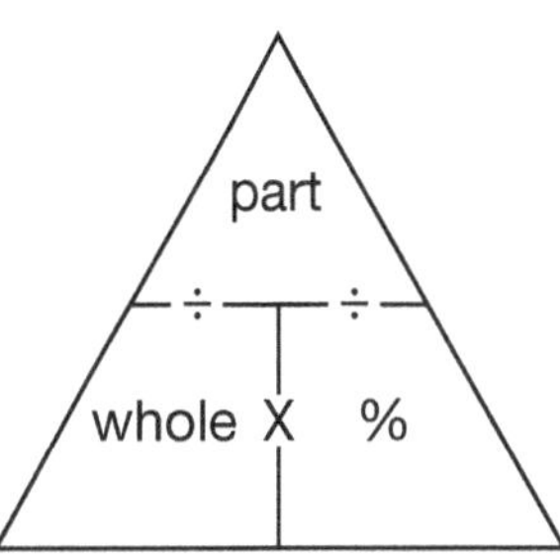

Find the Whole

Given:	the percent and the part
Equation:	Part ÷ Percent = Whole
Example:	36 is 75% of what number?
	36 ÷ 0.75 = 48

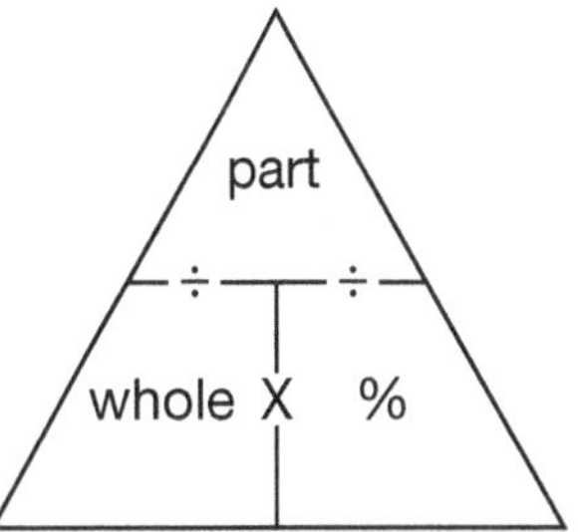

Glossary

compare (page 26)   determine which number is greater than the other or if the numbers are equal

decimal (page 62)   a number with one or more digits to the right of the decimal point; the numbers to the left of the decimal point are whole numbers, and the numbers to the right of the decimal point are values less than 1

decimal point (page 62)   a symbol used to separate the ones and tenths places in a decimal

denominator (page 12)   the number below the fraction bar in a fraction

difference (page 75)   the answer to a subtraction problem

digit (page 64)   one of the ten symbols used to write numbers

discount (page 112)   a cut in price

dividend (page 52)   the amount being divided

divisor (page 52)   the number you divide by

equation (page 110)   a statement of equality between two terms

equivalent (page 16)   equal or having the same value

equivalent fractions (page 16)   fractions that name the same amount

factor (page 18)   a whole number that evenly divides into another whole number

factors (page 18)   the numbers that are multiplied together to make another number

formula (page 114)   a rule that shows the relationship between two or more quantities; for example, the formula for calculating simple interest is $I = p \times r \times t$

fraction (page 10)   a number that names part of a whole or part of a group; usually the top number is smaller than the bottom one

greatest common factor (GCF) (page 18)   the greatest number that is a factor of two or more numbers; for example, the greatest common factor of 18 and 30 is 6

hundredth (page 62)   a decimal with two places to the right of the decimal point

improper fraction (page 30)   a fraction that has a numerator greater than or equal to the denominator; for example, $\frac{9}{5}$ or $\frac{11}{3}$

interest (I) (page 114)   the money paid for using or saving other money; the amount banks charge or pay on money borrowed or saved

interest rate (page 114)   the rate, given as a percent, used to determine interest; the percent a bank pays or charges on the principal

least common denominator (LCD) (page 24)   the smallest number that the denominators of fractions being added or subtracted divide into evenly

least common multiple (LCM) (page 22)   the smallest number that is a multiple of two or more other numbers

mixed number (page 28)   a number that contains both a whole number and a fraction; for example, $3\frac{1}{2}$ or $12\frac{3}{5}$

number line (page 22)   a line with equally spaced points that are labeled with numbers

numerator (page 12)   the number above the fraction bar in a fraction

percent (page 92)   a special ratio that compares a number to 100; another way of saying *per hundred*

percent equation (page 110)   an equation used to show and solve percent problems

place value (page 64)   the value of an individual digit depending upon its location within a greater number

place-value chart (page 64)   shows the value of each digit in a whole or decimal number by displaying each digit's location (tenths, hundredths, etc.)

principal (p) (page 114)   the amount of money you start with; for example, the original amount of a loan

probability (page 58)   the likelihood that something will happen

rate (r) (page 114)   the percent of interest paid on the principal

ratio (page 60)   compares two quantities, amounts, or numbers; ratios should be written in simplest form

reciprocal (page 52)   either of a pair of numbers whose product is 1; for example, $\frac{2}{3}$ and $\frac{3}{2}$ are reciprocals

rename (page 31)   change

simple interest (page 114)   money paid based only on the principal $(I = p \times r \times t)$

simplest form (page 20)   a fraction in which 1 is the only number that divides evenly into the numerator and denominator

tenth (page 62)   a decimal with one place to the right of the decimal point

time (t) (page 114)   the amount of time money is in the bank

variable (page 110)   a letter used to represent the number you are trying to find

ASSESSMENT

PAGES 4–8

Part 1: Fractions

1. $\frac{2}{5}$ 2. $\frac{3}{8}$ 3. $\frac{2}{3}$

4. $\frac{1}{2}$ 5. $\frac{3}{5}$ 6. $\frac{3}{4}$

7. $\frac{1}{3}$ 8. $\frac{1}{2}$ 9. 6

10. 4   11. 8   12. $\frac{3}{4} > \frac{3}{5}$

13. $\frac{3}{8} < \frac{2}{3}$ 14. $\frac{5}{10} = \frac{1}{2}$ 15. $\frac{7}{8} > \frac{5}{6}$

16. $\frac{1}{4} < \frac{1}{3}$ 17. $\frac{4}{8} = \frac{3}{6}$ 18. $1\frac{2}{5}$

19. 3   20. $2\frac{3}{4}$ 21. $\frac{3}{5}$

22. $\frac{1}{2}$ 23. $\frac{3}{5}$ 24. $\frac{7}{8}$

25. $\frac{1}{2}$ 26. $\frac{1}{10}$ 27. $3\frac{3}{4}$

28. $1\frac{2}{5}$ 29. $3\frac{7}{10}$ 30. $\frac{4}{15}$

31. $\frac{2}{3}$ 32. $\frac{1}{8}$ 33. $\frac{5}{6}$

34. $3\frac{9}{16}$ 35. $4\frac{4}{5}$ 36. $\frac{1}{2}$

37. $\frac{4}{3}$ 38. $\frac{1}{3}$

Part 2: Decimals

1. 4.4   2. 8.25   3. one tenth

4. two hundredths   5. 0.45 < 0.54   6. 0.10 > 0.01

7. 0.3 = 0.30   8. 0.27 > 0.26   9. 0.19 < 0.20

10. 1.5 = 1.50   11. 0.79   12. 0.52

13. 1.72   14. 1.6   15. 1.98

16. 1.71   17. $1.82   18. $3.59

19. $11.14   20. 1   21. 3.3

22. 27   23. 0.31   24. 2.52

25. 6.38   26. $8.33   27. $1.60

28. $16.25

Part 3: Percents

1. 47%   2. 85%   3. 123%

4. 35%   5. 19%   6. 250%

7. 0.54   8. 0.88   9. 0.02

10. 70%   11. 25%   12. 50%

13. $\frac{3}{10}$ 14. $\frac{4}{5}$ 15. $\frac{11}{20}$

16. 300   17. 63   18. 100

19. 40   20. 70%   21. 50%

Part 4: Word Problems

1. Ming   2. $\frac{2}{3}$ hour   3. 8 hours

4. $\frac{5}{8}$ 5. 8   6. 0.45 minute

7. 2 packages for $9.25

8. $2.00   9. 195   10. $312.00

Page 10

On Your Own

$\frac{1}{3}$

Page 11

1. $\frac{1}{2}$ 2. $\frac{1}{3}$ 3. $\frac{3}{4}$

4. $\frac{4}{5}$ 5. $\frac{1}{6}$ 6. $\frac{3}{8}$

7. $\frac{7}{10}$ 8. $\frac{1}{10}$

Page 12

On Your Own

$\frac{1}{4}$, one fourth

Page 13

1. $\frac{1}{4}$ 2. $\frac{1}{5}$ 3. $\frac{2}{3}$

4. $\frac{3}{8}$ 5. one fourth   6. four fifths

7. two thirds   8. five eighths   9. $\frac{7}{8}$, seven eighths

10. $\frac{5}{6}$, five sixths

Page 14

On Your Own

$\frac{5}{8}$, five eighths

Page 15

1. $\frac{1}{3}$ 2. $\frac{1}{4}$ 3. $\frac{3}{6}$

4. $\frac{7}{8}$ 5. $\frac{4}{5}$ 6. $\frac{1}{5}$

7. $\frac{2}{3}$, two thirds   8. $\frac{5}{8}$

Page 16

On Your Own

Answers may vary. $\frac{6}{9}$

Page 17

1. yes   2. no

3.–8. Answers may vary.

3. $\frac{6}{8}$ 4. $\frac{6}{10}$ 5. $\frac{3}{5}$

6. $\frac{6}{8}$ or $\frac{3}{4}$ 7. $\frac{9}{12}$; $\frac{3}{4}$ 8. $\frac{10}{16}$; $\frac{5}{8}$

Page 18

On Your Own

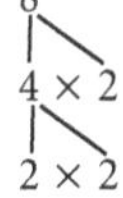

$4 = 2 \times 2$

$8 = 2 \times 2 \times 2$

$2 \times 2 = 4$

The greatest common factor of 4 and 8 is 4.

Page 19

1. 3; 3, 2; $3 \times 2 = 6$; The GCF is 6.

2. 2; 2, 2; $3 \times 2 = 6$; The GCF is 6.

3. 4   4. 3   5. 8

6. 5   7. 3, 6   8. 1, 2

Page 20

On Your Own

$\frac{1}{2}$

Page 21

1. $\frac{1}{3}$ 2. $\frac{4}{5}$ 3. 1

4. 4   5. $\frac{2}{3}$ 6. $\frac{1}{3}$

7. $\frac{1}{2}$ 8. $\frac{3}{4}$ 9. $\frac{1}{2}$

10. $\frac{2}{5}$

Page 22

On Your Own

The LCM is 15. Check students' number line.

Page 23

1. 6   2. 12   3. 20

4. 28   5. 6   6. 24

7. in 12 days   8. in 10 days

Page 24

On Your Own:

Multiples of 5: 5, 10, 15, 20, 25, 30, 35

Multiples of 2: 2, 4, 6, 8, 10, 12, 14

LCD = 10

$\frac{2}{5} = \frac{4}{10}$

$\frac{1}{2} = \frac{5}{10}$

Page 25

1. Find the LCM of 3 and 5.

   Multiples of 3: 3, 6, 9, 12, 15

   Multiples of 5: 5, 10, 15, 20, 25

   The LCM of 3 and 5 is 15.

   The LCD of $\frac{2}{3}$ and $\frac{3}{5}$ is 15.

   $\frac{2}{3} = \frac{2 \times 5}{3 \times 5} = \frac{10}{15}$

   $\frac{3}{5} = \frac{3 \times 3}{5 \times 3} = \frac{9}{15}$

2. Find the LCM of 4 and 3.

   Multiples of 4: 4, 8, 12, 16, 20

Multiples of 3: 3, 6, 9, 12, 15

The LCM of 4 and 3 is 12.

The LCD of $\frac{3}{4}$ and $\frac{1}{3}$ is 12.

$\frac{3}{4} = \frac{3 \times 3}{4 \times 3} = \frac{9}{12}$

$\frac{1}{3} = \frac{1 \times 4}{3 \times 4} = \frac{4}{12}$

3. Find the LCM of 2 and 3.

   Multiples of 2: 2, 4, 6, 8, 10

   Multiples of 3: 3, 6, 9, 12, 15

   The LCM of 2 and 3 is 6.

   The LCD of $\frac{1}{2}$ and $\frac{2}{3}$ is 6.

   $\frac{1}{2} = \frac{1 \times 3}{2 \times 3} = \frac{3}{6}$

   $\frac{2}{3} = \frac{2 \times 2}{3 \times 2} = \frac{4}{6}$

4. Find the LCM of 6 and 12.

   Multiples of 6: 6, 12, 18, 24, 30

   Multiples of 12: 12, 24, 36, 48, 60

   The LCM of 6 and 12 is 12.

   The LCD of $\frac{5}{6}$ and $\frac{1}{12}$ is 12.

   $\frac{5}{6} = \frac{5 \times 2}{6 \times 2} = \frac{10}{12}$

   $\frac{1}{12} = \frac{1 \times 1}{12 \times 1} = \frac{1}{12}$

5. Find the LCM of 7 and 2.

   Multiples of 7: 7, 14, 21, 28, 35, 42, 49

   Multiples of 2: 2, 4, 6, 8, 10, 12, 14

   The LCM of 7 and 2 is 14.

   The LCD of $\frac{2}{7}$ and $\frac{1}{2}$ is 14.

   $\frac{2}{7} = \frac{2 \times 2}{7 \times 2} = \frac{4}{14}$

   $\frac{1}{2} = \frac{1 \times 7}{2 \times 7} = \frac{7}{14}$

6. LCD = 12

   $\frac{2}{3} = \frac{2 \times 4}{3 \times 4} = \frac{8}{12}$

   $\frac{3}{4} = \frac{3 \times 3}{4 \times 3} = \frac{9}{12}$

7. LCD = 15

   $\frac{1}{3} = \frac{1 \times 5}{3 \times 5} = \frac{5}{15}$

   $\frac{2}{5} = \frac{2 \times 3}{5 \times 3} = \frac{6}{15}$

8. LCD = 30

   $\frac{5}{6} = \frac{5 \times 5}{6 \times 5} = \frac{25}{30}$

   $\frac{4}{5} = \frac{4 \times 6}{5 \times 6} = \frac{24}{30}$

Page 26

On Your Own

The LCD of $\frac{3}{5}$ and $\frac{2}{3}$ is 15.

$\frac{3}{5} = \frac{9}{15}$

$\frac{2}{3} = \frac{10}{15}$

$9 < 10$, so $\frac{9}{15} < \frac{10}{15}$, so $\frac{3}{5} < \frac{2}{3}$

Fractions, Decimals, and Percents: Answer Key
Strengthening Math Skills, SV 9781419039027

1. $\frac{1}{3} < \frac{2}{3}$ 2. $\frac{7}{8} > \frac{3}{4}$ 3. $\frac{4}{5} > \frac{3}{5}$
4. $\frac{1}{4} < \frac{2}{4}$ 5. $\frac{1}{2} > \frac{1}{5}$ 6. $\frac{1}{3} > \frac{1}{4}$
7. $\frac{5}{6} > \frac{3}{4}$ 8. $\frac{3}{8} < \frac{3}{4}$
9. $\frac{2}{3} < \frac{3}{4}$, so Monroe studied longer.
10. $\frac{1}{2} < \frac{3}{5} < \frac{7}{10}$, so Cho rode the farthest.

Page 28

On Your Own

$1\frac{3}{4}$

Page 29

1. $1\frac{3}{5}$ 2. $2\frac{1}{6}$ 3. $3\frac{1}{2}$
4. $2\frac{5}{8}$ 5. $2\frac{1}{6}$ 6. $1\frac{7}{10}$

Page 30

On Your Own

$\frac{7}{2} = 3\frac{1}{2}$

Page 31

1. $1\frac{1}{2}$ 2. $2\frac{1}{3}$ 3. $2\frac{3}{4}$
4. $1\frac{4}{5}$ 5. $2\frac{1}{6}$ 6. $1\frac{7}{8}$
7. $2\frac{1}{2}$ 8. 2 9. $1\frac{3}{4}$
10. $1\frac{1}{2}$ 11. $\frac{11}{2}, 5\frac{1}{2}$ 12. 5

Page 32

On Your Own

$2\frac{2}{3} = \frac{8}{3}$

Page 33

1. $\frac{5}{2}$ 2. $\frac{21}{5}$ 3. $\frac{7}{4}$
4. $\frac{7}{1}$ 5. $\frac{11}{8}$ 6. $\frac{18}{5}$
7. $\frac{11}{10}$ 8. $\frac{10}{1}$ 9. $\frac{27}{5}$
10. $\frac{9}{4}$ 11. $\frac{11}{2}$ 12. $\frac{7}{2}$
13. $\frac{5}{4}$ 14. $\frac{13}{8}$

Page 34

On Your Own

$\frac{1}{4} + \frac{1}{4} = \frac{2}{4} = \frac{1}{2}$

Page 35

1. $\frac{3}{4}$ 2. $\frac{5}{6}$ 3. $\frac{5}{8}$
4. $\frac{4}{5}$ 5. $\frac{5}{8}$ 6. $\frac{2}{3}$
7. $\frac{3}{6} = \frac{1}{2}$ 8. $\frac{6}{9} = \frac{2}{3}$ 9. $\frac{6}{7}$
10. $\frac{7}{8}$ 11. $\frac{5}{6}$ 12. $\frac{6}{7}$

Page 36

On Your Own

The LCD of $\frac{1}{5}$ and $\frac{1}{2}$ is 10.

$\frac{1}{5} = \frac{2}{10}$

$\frac{1}{2} = \frac{5}{10}$

$\frac{2}{10} + \frac{5}{10} = \frac{7}{10}$

So, $\frac{1}{5} + \frac{1}{2} = \frac{7}{10}$

Page 37

1. The LCD is 4.   2. The LCD is 9.   3. The LCD is 12.

4. $\frac{2}{6} = \frac{4}{12}$ 5. $\frac{1}{2} = \frac{4}{8}$
$\frac{1}{4} = \frac{3}{12}$ $\frac{3}{8} = \frac{3}{8}$
$\frac{4}{12} + \frac{3}{12} = \frac{7}{12}$ $\frac{4}{8} + \frac{3}{8} = \frac{7}{8}$
So, $\frac{2}{6} + \frac{1}{4} = \frac{7}{12}$ So, $\frac{1}{2} + \frac{3}{8} = \frac{7}{8}$

6. $\frac{2}{5} = \frac{6}{15}$ 7. $\frac{2}{3} = \frac{4}{6}$
$\frac{1}{3} = \frac{5}{15}$ $\frac{1}{2} = \frac{3}{6}$
$\frac{6}{15} + \frac{5}{15} = \frac{11}{15}$ $\frac{4}{6} + \frac{3}{6} = \frac{7}{6} = 1\frac{1}{6}$
So, $\frac{2}{5} + \frac{1}{3} = \frac{11}{15}$ So, $\frac{2}{3} + \frac{1}{2} = 1\frac{1}{6}$

8. $\frac{5}{8} = \frac{5}{8}$ 9. $\frac{5}{6} = \frac{5}{6}$
$\frac{3}{4} = \frac{6}{8}$ $\frac{2}{3} = \frac{4}{6}$
$\frac{5}{8} + \frac{6}{8} = \frac{11}{8} = 1\frac{3}{8}$ $\frac{5}{6} + \frac{4}{6} = \frac{9}{6} = 1\frac{3}{6} = 1\frac{1}{2}$
So, $\frac{5}{8} + \frac{3}{4} = 1\frac{3}{8}$ So, $\frac{5}{6} + \frac{2}{3} = 1\frac{1}{2}$

10. $\frac{5}{6}$ hour   11. $\frac{7}{6} = 1\frac{1}{6}$ hours   12. $\frac{7}{10}$

Page 38

On Your Own

$3\frac{5}{8} + 2\frac{1}{8} = 5\frac{6}{8} = 5\frac{3}{4}$

Page 39

1. $7\frac{3}{5}$ 2. $8\frac{6}{10} = 8\frac{3}{5}$ 3. $9\frac{1}{4}$
4. 4 5. $4\frac{8}{10} + 5\frac{5}{10} = 9\frac{13}{10} = 9 + 1\frac{3}{10} = 10\frac{3}{10}$
6. $2\frac{2}{12} + 3\frac{7}{12} = 5\frac{9}{12} = 5\frac{3}{4}$
7. $1\frac{5}{12} + 6\frac{2}{12} = 7\frac{7}{12}$ 8. $8\frac{2}{9} + 1\frac{3}{9} = 9\frac{5}{9}$
9. $1\frac{8}{12} + 5\frac{9}{12} + 4\frac{10}{12} = 10\frac{27}{12} = 10 + 2\frac{3}{12} = 12\frac{3}{12} = 12\frac{1}{4}$
10. $4\frac{4}{10} + 5\frac{5}{10} = 9\frac{9}{10}$
11. $1\frac{3}{12} + 1\frac{4}{12} = 2\frac{7}{12}$
12. $15\frac{3}{6} + 16\frac{5}{6} = 31\frac{8}{6} = 31 + 1\frac{2}{6} = 32\frac{2}{6} = 32\frac{1}{3}$

Page 40

On Your Own

$\frac{5}{8} - \frac{3}{8} = \frac{2}{8} = \frac{1}{4}$

Page 41

1. $\frac{1}{4}$ 2. $\frac{4}{6} = \frac{2}{3}$ 3. $\frac{3}{8}$
4. $\frac{3}{7}$ 5. $\frac{4}{8} = \frac{1}{2}$ 6. $\frac{3}{9} = \frac{1}{3}$
7. $\frac{3}{5}$ 8. $\frac{4}{10} = \frac{2}{5}$ 9. $\frac{6}{12} = \frac{1}{2}$
10. $\frac{3}{10}$ of a mile   11. $\frac{2}{8}$ inch $= \frac{1}{4}$ inch
12. $\frac{8}{8} - \frac{3}{8} = \frac{5}{8} - \frac{5}{8} = \frac{0}{8} = 0$ pieces left

Page 42

On Your Own

The LCD of $\frac{4}{5}$ and $\frac{3}{10}$ is 10.

$\frac{4}{5} = \frac{8}{10}$

$\frac{3}{10} = \frac{3}{10}$

$\frac{8}{10} - \frac{3}{10} = \frac{5}{10} = \frac{1}{2}$

So, $\frac{4}{5} - \frac{3}{10} = \frac{1}{2}$

Page 43

1. $\frac{9}{14} - \frac{6}{14} = \frac{3}{14}$
2. $\frac{11}{12} - \frac{9}{12} = \frac{2}{12} = \frac{1}{6}$
3. $\frac{20}{24} - \frac{15}{24} = \frac{5}{24}$
4. $\frac{9}{16} - \frac{2}{16} = \frac{7}{16}$
5. $\frac{7}{10} - \frac{5}{10} = \frac{2}{10} = \frac{1}{5}$
6. $\frac{6}{9} - \frac{4}{9} = \frac{2}{9}$
7. $\frac{3}{6} - \frac{2}{6} = \frac{1}{6}$
8. $\frac{4}{12} - \frac{3}{12} = \frac{1}{12}$
9. $\frac{3}{9} - \frac{3}{9} = 0$
10. $\frac{18}{20} - \frac{15}{20} = \frac{3}{20}$ of a mile
11. $\frac{9}{12} - \frac{8}{12} = \frac{1}{12}$ of an hour
12. $\frac{21}{24} - \frac{20}{24} = \frac{1}{24}$ of a yard

Page 44

On Your Own

$3\frac{3}{4} = 3\frac{3}{4}$

$1\frac{1}{2} = 1\frac{2}{4}$

$3\frac{3}{4} - 1\frac{2}{4} = 2\frac{1}{4}$

So, $3\frac{3}{4} - 1\frac{1}{2} = 2\frac{1}{4}$

Page 45

1. $1\frac{1}{4}$
2. $7\frac{4}{6} = 7\frac{2}{3}$
3. $9\frac{4}{12} = 9\frac{1}{3}$
4. $2\frac{9}{8} - 2\frac{5}{8} = \frac{4}{8} = \frac{1}{2}$
5. $3\frac{5}{4} - 2\frac{3}{4} = 1\frac{2}{4} = 1\frac{1}{2}$
6. $6\frac{2}{2} - 5\frac{1}{2} = 1\frac{1}{2}$
7. $7\frac{4}{9} - 2\frac{3}{9} = 5\frac{1}{9}$
8. $5\frac{2}{10} - 1\frac{3}{10} = 4\frac{12}{10} - 1\frac{3}{10} = 3\frac{9}{10}$
9. $5\frac{3}{6} - 2\frac{5}{6} = 4\frac{9}{6} - 2\frac{5}{6} = 2\frac{4}{6} = 2\frac{2}{3}$
10. $1\frac{1}{3}$ miles
11. $2\frac{1}{4} - 1\frac{2}{4} = 1\frac{5}{4} - 1\frac{2}{4} = \frac{3}{4}$ ounce
12. $\frac{3}{6}$ pound $= \frac{1}{2}$ pound

Page 46

On Your Own

$\frac{1}{2} \times \frac{4}{8} = \frac{1 \times 4}{2 \times 8} = \frac{4}{16} = \frac{1}{4}$

Page 47

1. $\frac{1}{8}$
2. $\frac{2}{9}$
3. $\frac{2}{15}$
4. $\frac{3}{8}$
5. $\frac{14}{24} = \frac{7}{12}$
6. $\frac{3}{24} = \frac{1}{8}$
7. $\frac{2}{20} = \frac{1}{10}$
8. $\frac{8}{25}$
9. $\frac{10}{21}$
10. $\frac{4}{5} \times \frac{1}{2} = \frac{4}{10} = \frac{2}{5}$ cup
11. $\frac{1}{2} \times \frac{1}{3} = \frac{1}{6}$
12. $\frac{3}{4} \times \frac{2}{3} = \frac{6}{12} = \frac{1}{2}$ mile

Page 48

On Your Own

$\frac{1}{2} \times 8 = \frac{1}{2} \times \frac{8}{1} = \frac{1 \times 8}{2 \times 1} = \frac{8}{2} = 4$

Page 49

1. $\frac{1}{4} \times \frac{16}{1} = \frac{16}{4} = 4$
2. $\frac{1}{3} \times \frac{12}{1} = \frac{12}{3} = 4$
3. $\frac{1}{7} \times \frac{21}{1} = \frac{21}{7} = 3$
4. $\frac{3}{4} \times \frac{6}{1} = \frac{18}{4} = \frac{9}{2} = 4\frac{1}{2}$
5. $\frac{3}{5} \times \frac{7}{1} = \frac{21}{5} = 4\frac{1}{5}$
6. $\frac{15}{1} \times \frac{2}{3} = \frac{30}{3} = 10$
7. $\frac{6}{1} \times \frac{4}{5} = \frac{24}{5} = 4\frac{4}{5}$
8. $\frac{3}{8} \times \frac{11}{1} = \frac{33}{8} = 4\frac{1}{8}$
9. $\frac{5}{6} \times \frac{5}{1} = \frac{25}{6} = 4\frac{1}{6}$
10. $\frac{9}{1} \times \frac{1}{3} = \frac{9}{3} = 3$
11. $\frac{20}{1} \times \frac{3}{4} = \frac{60}{4} = 15$ yards
12. $\frac{24}{1} \times \frac{2}{3} = \frac{48}{3} = 16$

Page 50

On Your Own

$\frac{1}{3} \times 2\frac{1}{4} = \frac{1}{3} \times \frac{9}{4} = \frac{9 \times 1}{3 \times 4} = \frac{9}{12} = \frac{3}{4}$

Page 51

1. $\frac{1}{3} \times \frac{16}{5} = \frac{16}{15} = 1\frac{1}{15}$
2. $\frac{1}{6} \times \frac{9}{2} = \frac{9}{12} = \frac{3}{4}$
3. $\frac{1}{2} \times \frac{10}{3} = \frac{10}{6} = \frac{5}{3} = 1\frac{2}{3}$
4. $\frac{1}{3} \times \frac{7}{2} = \frac{7}{6} = 1\frac{1}{6}$
5. $\frac{1}{4} \times \frac{17}{6} = \frac{17}{24}$
6. $\frac{2}{3} \times \frac{9}{5} = \frac{18}{15} = \frac{6}{5} = 1\frac{1}{5}$
7. $\frac{3}{4} \times \frac{5}{3} = \frac{15}{12} = \frac{5}{4} = 1\frac{1}{4}$
8. $\frac{5}{2} \times \frac{2}{5} = \frac{10}{10} = 1$
9. $\frac{5}{6} \times \frac{28}{5} = \frac{140}{30} = \frac{14}{3} = 4\frac{2}{3}$
10. $\frac{3}{4} \times \frac{3}{2} = \frac{9}{8} = 1\frac{1}{8}$ miles
11. $\frac{4}{5} \times \frac{9}{4} = \frac{36}{20} = \frac{9}{5} = 1\frac{4}{5}$ cups
12. $\frac{2}{3} \times \frac{5}{2} = \frac{10}{6} = \frac{5}{3} = 1\frac{2}{3}$ cups

Page 52

On Your Own

$\frac{2}{3} \div \frac{1}{3} = \frac{2}{3} \times \frac{3}{1} = \frac{2 \times 3}{3 \times 1} = \frac{6}{3} = 2$

Page 53

1. $\frac{4}{1}$
2. $\frac{8}{3}$
3. $\frac{2}{5}$
4. $\frac{2}{4} \times \frac{8}{1} = \frac{16}{4} = 4$
5. $\frac{1}{3} \times \frac{5}{2} = \frac{5}{6}$
6. $\frac{3}{4} \times \frac{2}{1} = \frac{6}{4} = \frac{3}{2} = 1\frac{1}{2}$
7. $\frac{3}{5} \times \frac{5}{1} = \frac{15}{5} = 3$
8. $\frac{2}{3} \times \frac{3}{2} = \frac{6}{6} = 1$
9. $\frac{7}{10} \times \frac{1}{2} = \frac{7}{20}$
10. $\frac{3}{4} \times \frac{8}{1} = \frac{24}{4} = 6$ invitations
11. $\frac{3}{4} \times \frac{3}{1} = \frac{9}{4} = 2\frac{1}{4}$ dozen
12. $\frac{2}{3} \times \frac{6}{1} = \frac{12}{3} = 4$ pieces

Page 55

1. $\frac{1}{2}$ hour
2. $\frac{3}{4}$ hour
3. $1\frac{1}{2}$ hours
4. $1\frac{1}{4}$ hours
5. 15 minutes $= \frac{1}{4}$ hour
6. 1 hour 45 minutes $= 1\frac{3}{4}$ hour
7. $\frac{2}{3}$ hour $= 40$ minutes
8. 5:00

Page 56

On Your Own

$2\frac{3}{4}$ inches long

Page 57

1. $1\frac{1}{2}$ inches
2. $2\frac{1}{8}$ inches
3. $3\frac{3}{4}$ inches
4. Check length.
5. Check length.
6. Check length.
7. $6\frac{1}{4}$; $12\frac{3}{8}$; $14\frac{11}{12}$
8. $9\frac{5}{4} - 3\frac{3}{4} = 6\frac{2}{4} = 6\frac{1}{2}$ feet

Fractions, Decimals, and Percents: Answer Key
Strengthening Math Skills, SV 9781419039027

Page 58

On Your Own

$\frac{1}{6}$

Page 59

1. $\frac{1}{4}$

2. $\frac{1}{2}$

3. $\frac{1}{8}$

4. $\frac{1}{8}$

5. $\frac{3}{10}$

6. $\frac{1}{5}$

7. $\frac{1}{5}$

8. $\frac{1}{10}$

9. $\frac{2}{11}$

10. $\frac{6}{15} = \frac{2}{5}$

Page 60

On Your Own

$\frac{1}{4}$

Page 61

1. $\frac{3}{6} = \frac{1}{2}$

2. $\frac{4}{7}$

3. $\frac{4}{5}$

4. $\frac{2}{3}$

5. $\frac{6}{8} = \frac{3}{4}$

6. $\frac{10}{25} = \frac{2}{5}$

7. $\frac{5}{10} = \frac{1}{2}$

8. $\frac{4}{12} = \frac{1}{3}$

9. $\frac{8}{12} = \frac{2}{3}$

10. $\frac{4}{12} = \frac{1}{3}$

Page 62

On Your Own

0.3, three tenths

Page 63

1. 0.1, one tenth

2. 0.7, seven tenths

3. 0.23, twenty-three hundredths

4. 0.77, seventy-seven hundredths

5. Check the shading.

6. Check the shading.

7. 0.71, seventy-one hundredths

Page 64

On Your Own

1, 5, 6, 7

15.67 = 1 ten + 5 ones + 6 tenths + 7 hundredths = fifteen and sixty-seven hundredths

Page 65

1. Check place-value chart.

   7 ones + 3 tenths

   seven and three tenths

2. Check place-value chart.

   4 tens + 7 ones + 1 tenth + 7 hundredths

   forty-seven and seventeen hundredths

3. 13.23; check place-value chart.

4. 95.61; check place-value chart.

5. 3.5

6. 26.3

7. 2.6

8. 5.25

Page 66

On Your Own

$\frac{1}{2} \times \frac{5}{5} = \frac{5}{10}$ = five tenths = 0.5

$1 \div 2 = 0.5$

Page 67

1. 0.3, three tenths

2. 0.17, seventeen hundredths

3. 0.4, four tenths

4. 0.75, seventy-five hundredths

5. 0.55, fifty-five hundredths

6. 0.9

7. 0.35

8. 0.6

Page 68

On Your Own

3.5

Page 69

1. 7

2. 3

3. 2

4. 3

5. 1

6. 5

7. 8.9

8. 1.4

9. 3.9

10. 2.8

11. 7.5

12. 4.1

13. 24.51

14. 7 inches

15. 5.5 inches

Page 70

On Your Own

9.91 > 9.90

Page 71

1. 1.8 > 1.5

2. 3.3 = 3.30

3. 4.51 > 4.5

4. 13.45 < 13.54

5. 21.01 < 21.10

6. 55.55 < 55.56

7. 6.8 > 6.76

8. 11.12 < 11.21

9. 1.75 > 1.7, so the red jar holds more.

10. 0.17 < 0.20 < 0.27, so Tucson had the least rainfall.

Page 72

On Your Own

0.4 + 1.5 = 1.9

Page 73

1. 0.9

2. 1.3

3. 3.14

4. 1.4

5. 1.25

6. 1.2

7. 2.35

8. 10.79

9. 12.61

10. 4.00 miles

11. 8.15 quarts

12. 14.10 yards

Page 74

On Your Own

3.6 − 1.5 = 2.1

Page 75

1. 0.6

2. 0.14

3. 0.73

4. 0.08

5. 1.04

6. 0.42

7. 3.01	**8.** 6.25	**9.** 2.25
10. 3.75 gallons	**11.** 1.24 meters	**12.** 8.50 ounces

Page 76

On Your Own

$5.6 \times 3 = 16.8$

Page 77

1. 0.76	**2.** 25.32	**3.** 8.61
4. 27.10	**5.** 20.55	**6.** 0.66
7. 6.0	**8.** 4.0	**9.** 19.98
10. 5.0	**11.** 19.5 hours	**12.** 16.25 yards

Page 78

On Your Own

$7.89 \times 10 = 78.9$

Page 79

1. 136.5, 1,365.0	**2.** 832.0, 8,320.0	**3.** 10.1
4. 28.2	**5.** 3,937.0	**6.** 67.5
7. 2,001.0	**8.** 0.4	**9.** 45.4
10. 1,331.0	**11.** 125.0 inches	**12.** 6.5 ounces

Page 80

On Your Own

$1.2 \times 2.1 = 2.52$

Page 81

1. 0.975	**2.** 4.347	**3.** 4.90
4. 12.231	**5.** 2.53	**6.** 23.256
7. 0.63	**8.** 4.35	**9.** 22.475
10. 2.912	**11.** 5.625 square feet	
12. 459.65 miles		

Page 82

On Your Own

$0.52 \times 0.11 = 0.0572$

Page 83

1. 0.026	**2.** 0.024	**3.** 1.016
4. 0.06	**5.** 0.033	**6.** 0.042
7. 0.011	**8.** 0.100	**9.** 0.0644
10. 0.078	**11.** 0.025 kilometer	
12. 0.09 quart		

Page 84

On Your Own

$3.24 \div 4 = 0.81$

Page 85

1. 0.78	**2.** 2.08	**3.** 3.05
4. 1.6	**5.** 0.9	**6.** 1.1

7. 0.99	**8.** 3.06	**9.** 4.09
10. 4.25 cups	**11.** 4.5 ounces	**12.** 1.25 yards

Page 86

On Your Own

$8.75 \div 10 = 0.875$

Page 87

1. 0.75, 0.075	**2.** 0.333, 0.0333	**3.** 1.1
4. 2.32	**5.** 0.3793	**6.** 0.076
7. 0.345	**8.** 0.1743	**9.** 0.0387
10. 0.005	**11.** 0.355 gram	**12.** 19.55 inches

Page 88

On Your Own

$\$1.43 + \$2.95 = \$4.38$

Page 89

1. $5.50	**2.** $8.15	**3.** $24.00
4. $4.42	**5.** $14.37	**6.** $0.80
7. $45.26	**8.** $0.99	**9.** $26.01

10. $14.78 + $16.49 = $31.27

11. $78.90 − $25.25 = $53.65

12. $15.65 + $22.75 + $19.15 = $57.55

Page 90

On Your Own

$\$6.50 \div 2 = \$3.25$

Page 91

1. $9.75	**2.** $22.00	**3.** $1.50
4. $1.10	**5.** $2.72	**6.** $0.35
7. $107.10	**8.** $7.16	**9.** $61.90

10. $2.59 × 2 = $5.18

11. $5.55 ÷ 3 = $1.85

12. $0.85 × 5 = $4.25

Page 92

On Your Own

$\frac{31}{100}$, 31%

Page 93

1. 17%	**2.** 0.89, 89%	**3.** $\frac{63}{100}$, 63%
4. 13%	**5.** 77%	**6.** 9%
7. $\frac{41}{100}$, 41%	**8.** 83%	

Page 94

On Your Own

$50\% \text{ of } 14 = \frac{14}{1} \times \frac{1}{2} = \frac{14}{2} = 7$

Page 95

1. divide
2. 50%
3. $\frac{2}{10}$ or $\frac{1}{5}$
4. 200; $2 \times 100 = 200$
5. 5; $10 \div 2 = 5$
6. 3; $30 \times \frac{1}{10} = \frac{30}{10} = 3$
7. 5
8. 1
9. 2
10. 25
11. 25
12. 30
13. $40 \times \frac{1}{2} = 20$ stamps; $40 \div 2 = 20$ stamps
14. $50 \times \frac{1}{10} = 5$ CDs; $50 \div 10 = 5$ CDs
15. $32 \times \frac{1}{4} = 8$ clocks; $32 \div 4 = 8$ clocks

Page 96

On Your Own

$0.83 \times 100 = 83.0 = 83\%$

Page 97

1. 75%
2. 12%
3. 41%
4. 60%
5. 90%
6. 30%
7. 2%
8. 8%
9. 4%
10. 115%
11. 227%
12. 350%
13. $0.87 = \frac{87}{100} = 87\%$
14. $0.33 = \frac{33}{100} = 33\%$
15. $1.0 - 0.3 = 0.7 = 0.70 = \frac{70}{100} = 70\%$

Page 98

On Your Own

$20\% = 0.20$

Page 99

1. 0.84
2. 0.19
3. 0.43
4. 0.05
5. 0.01
6. 0.09
7. 0.14
8. 0.40
9. 0.035
10. 1.25
11. 1.00
12. 2.50
13. 0.50
14. 0.80
15. 1.50

Page 100

On Your Own

$\frac{9}{10} = 0.90 = 90\%$

Page 101

1. $\frac{5}{10} = 0.50 = 50\%$
2. 77%
3. 33%
4. $\frac{10}{5} = 2.00 = 200\%$
5. $\frac{3}{5} = 0.60 = 60\%$
6. $\frac{15}{20} = 0.75 = 75\%$
7. $\frac{1}{4} = 0.25 = 25\%$
8. $\frac{1}{5} = 0.20 = 20\%$
9. $\frac{3}{4} = 0.75 = 75\%$
10. $\frac{6}{10} = 0.60 = 60\%$
11. $\frac{2}{5} = 0.40 = 40\%$
12. $\frac{25}{50} = 0.50 = 50\%$

Page 102

On Your Own

$60\% = \frac{60}{100} = \frac{6}{10} = \frac{3}{5}$

Page 103

1. $\frac{10}{100} = \frac{1}{10}$
2. $\frac{50}{100} = \frac{1}{2}$
3. $\frac{25}{100} = \frac{1}{4}$
4. $\frac{100}{100} = 1$
5. $\frac{66}{100} = \frac{33}{50}$
6. $\frac{8}{100} = \frac{2}{25}$
7. $\frac{75}{100} = \frac{3}{4}$
8. $\frac{48}{100} = \frac{12}{25}$
9. $\frac{55}{100} = \frac{11}{20}$
10. $\frac{1}{100}$
11. $\frac{120}{100} = \frac{6}{5} = 1\frac{1}{5}$
12. $\frac{250}{100} = \frac{5}{2} = 2\frac{1}{2}$
13. $\frac{35}{100} = \frac{7}{20}$
14. $\frac{40}{100} = \frac{2}{5}$
15. $\frac{85}{100} = \frac{17}{20}$

Page 104

On Your Own

part = whole × percent

part = $50 \times 40\%$

$40\% = 0.40$

$50 \times 0.40 = 20$

So, 40% of 50 is 20.

Page 105

1. $32 \times 0.25 = 8$
2. $40 \times 0.05 = 2$
3. $50 \times 0.60 = 30$
4. $90 \times 0.10 = 9$
5. $100 \times 0.50 = 50$
6. $200 \times 0.35 = 70$
7. $90 \times 0.90 = 81$
8. $400 \times 0.15 = 60$
9. $48 \times 1.50 = 72$
10. $1 \times 1.00 = 1$
11. $70 \times 0.60 = 42$ cars
12. $88 \times 0.75 = 66$ strikes

Page 106

On Your Own

whole = part ÷ percent

whole = $20 \div 40\%$

$40\% = 0.40$

$20 \div 0.40 = 50$

So, 20 is 40% of 50.

Page 107

1. $6 \div 0.10 = 60$
2. $10 \div 0.20 = 50$
3. $15 \div 0.25 = 60$
4. $25 \div 0.50 = 50$
5. $75 \div 0.75 = 100$
6. $30 \div 0.40 = 75$
7. $8 \div 0.40 = 20$ students
8. $18 \div 0.60 = 30$ people
9. $112 \div 0.80 = 140$ acres
10. $1{,}428 \div 1.19 = 1{,}200$ people

Page 108

On Your Own

percent = (part ÷ whole) × 100

percent = $(20 \div 80) \times 100$

$(20 \div 80) \times 100 = 0.25 \times 100 = 25\%$

So, 20 is 25% of 80.

Page 109

1. $40 \div 100 = 0.40 \times 100 = 40\%$

2. $90 \div 90 = 1 \times 100 = 100\%$

3. $15 \div 20 = 0.75 \times 100 = 75\%$

4. $1 \div 50 = 0.02 \times 100 = 2\%$

5. $48 \div 80 = 0.60 \times 100 = 60\%$

6. $50 \div 200 = 0.25 \times 100 = 25\%$

7. $72 \div 90 = 0.80 \times 100 = 80\%$

8. $36 \div 450 = 0.08 \times 100 = 8\%$

9. $240 \div 800 = 0.30 \times 100 = 30\%$

10. $56 \div 224 = 0.25 \times 100 = 25\%$

Page 110

On Your Own

30 is what percent of 120?

percent = (part $\div$ whole) $\times$ 100

$n = (30 \div 120) \times 100 = 0.25 \times 100$

$n = 25\%$

Page 111

1. $n = 50 \times 10\%$

2. $24 = 60 \times n$

3. $n = 80 \times 30\%$

4. $16 = n \times 80\%$

5. $n = 16 \times 25\%$; 4

6. $9 = 12 \times n$; 75%

7. $n = 80 \times 80\%$; 64

8. $15 = n \times 10\%$; 150

9. $n = (4 \div 10) \times 100$; 40%

10. $12 = n \times 15\%$; 80 coins

Page 112

On Your Own

$\$150 \times 0.30 = \$45$

$\$150 - \$45 = \$105$

Page 113

1. $1.20, $21.20

2. $0.38, $9.88

3. $12.50, $262.50

4. $3.99, $60.99

5. $1.50, $8.50

6. $3.30, $29.70

7. $78.00, $117.00

8. $19.25, $57.75

9. $\$16.00 \times 0.15 = \$2.40$; $\$16.00 - \$2.40 = \$13.60$; $\$13.60 \times 0.05 = \$0.68$; $\$13.60 + \$0.68 = \$14.28$

10. $\$40.00 \times 0.24 = \$9.60$; $\$40.00 - \$9.60 = \$30.40$; $\$30.40 \times 0.05 = \$1.52$; $\$30.40 + \$1.52 = \$31.92$

Page 114

On Your Own

$I = p \times r \times t$

$I = \$500.00 \times 3\% \times 1 \text{ year}$

$I = \$500.00 \times 0.03 \times 1$

$I = \$15.00$

Principal + Interest = Total amount

$\$500.00 + \$15.00 = \$515.00$

Page 115

1. $\$1,000 \times 0.06 \times 1 = \$60.00$

2. $\$100 \times 0.04 \times 2 = \$8.00$

3. $\$1,500 \times 0.05 \times 0.5 = \$37.50$

4. $\$800 \times 0.03 \times 0.25 = \$6.00$

5. $\$750 \times 0.07 \times 1 = \$52.50$; $\$750.00 + \$52.50 = \$802.50$

6. $\$3,000 \times 0.035 \times 3 = \$315.00$; $\$3,000.00 + \$315.00 = \$3,315.00$

7. $\$10,000 \times 0.06 \times 0.5 = \$300.00$; $\$10,000 + \$300.00 = \$10,300.00$

8. $\$2,000 \times 0.045 \times 4 = \$360.00$; $\$2,000.00 + \$360.00 = \$2,360.00$

9. $\$5,000 \times 0.05 \times 3 = \$750.00$; $\$5,000.00 + \$750.00 = \$5,750.00$

10. $\$350 \times 0.03 \times 2 = \$21.00$; $\$350.00 + \$21.00 = \$371.00$